AFFILIATE CONTENT SECRETS

AFFILIATE CONTENT SECRETS

PROVEN AFFILIATE MARKETING TIPS & STRATEGIES YOU CAN USE TO MAXIMIZE YOUR EARNINGS

STEPHEN HOCKMAN

BLUE HOUSE
BRANDS LLC

AFFILIATE CONTENT SECRETS
PROVEN AFFILIATE MARKETING TIPS & STRATEGIES
YOU CAN USE TO MAXIMIZE YOUR EARNINGS

Copyright © 2020 Blue House Brands LLC
Published in the United States of America by Blue House Brands LLC.
For more information visit: bluehousebrands.com

All rights reserved. No part of this book may be reproduced by any mechanical, photographic, or electronic process, or in the form of phonographic recording; nor may it be stored in a retrieval system, transmitted, or otherwise copied for public or private use—other than for "fair use" as brief quotations embodied in articles and reviews—without prior written permission of the publisher.

Disclaimer: The information provided in this book is for informational purposes only and is based on the author's personal experience. This book is not intended to be a definitive guide or to take the place of advice from a qualified professional. The publisher and the author do not make any guarantee or other promise as to any results that may be obtained from using the content of this book. The publisher and the author are providing this book and its contents on an "as is" basis and assume no responsibility for your actions. Your use of the information in this book is at your own risk.

ISBN 978-0-578-72877-3

FIRST EDITION

CONTENTS

Introduction...1

Affiliate Writing Secrets..9

Secret #1: Identify Your Target Buyer Persona...........................15

Secret #2: Act Like an Authority...23

Secret #3: Write Directly to Your Readers..................................29

Secret #4: Bond with Your Audience...33

Secret #5: Choose Active Voice Over Passive Voice..................37

Secret #6: Use Power Words..41

Secret #7: Write Like a 7th Grader (Or Even a 3rd Grader)........45

Secret #8: Use One Sentence Paragraphs (At Most Two)............51

Secret #9: Vary Your Sentence Length..55

Secret #10: Ask Rhetorical Questions..59

Secret #11: Use Expert Words..67

Secret #12: Quote Someone..77

Secret #13: Label Your Readers with a Noun..............................83

Secret #14: Bait Your Readers with a Hook................................91

Secret #15: Push Your Visitors to Read More.............................99

Secret #16: Pick 3 Products to Be Your All-Stars.....................105

Secret #17: Apply the Feature Stacking Trick...........................109

Secret #18: Focus on the Person, Not the Product....................115

Secret #19: Always Start with the Strongest Benefits...............121

Secret #20: Keep Your Negatives Brief.....................................123

Secret #21: If You Give a Strong Why, More People Will Buy.........127

Secret #22: Keep Referring Back to Your All-Stars...........................133

Secret #23: Take Advantage of Cross-Selling......................................137

Secret #24: Use the Power of Fluency, Frequency and Exposure.......141

Secret #25: Capture More Clicks with Irresistible Headlines.............151

Affiliate Page Structure Secrets...159

Secret Page Structure #1..163

Secret Page Structure #2..173

Conclusion..179

Next Steps...185

About the Author..187

INTRODUCTION

On April 24, 2019, I finally did it.

I quit my job as a Digital Marketing Director for a college and went full-time as an affiliate marketer. I no longer had to report to a boss, punch a time clock, or do work that wasn't making me happy. But most importantly, I no longer had a cap on my salary—I could literally earn as much money as I wanted to now that I had all of the time in the world to put into my affiliate sites.

Finally, I felt free to enjoy working on my terms.

But the road that led to this success didn't happen overnight.

In fact, my journey with affiliate marketing began in 2008 when I stumbled across the *30 Day Challenge* by Ed Dale. It was an online course that taught you how to set up and rank a website that could make you passive income online. The goal was to make your first dollar within 30 days without spending any money to earn it.

And the process that Ed taught worked!

I remember setting up my first site on a free blogging platform and writing my first article about Bose headphones. At the time, I was interested in noise-canceling headphones and Bose made some of the best ones available. So I signed up for Amazon's Associate Program which allowed me to earn a commission on the sale of products if someone bought them through my affiliate links.

I then put together a web page that talked about the pros and cons of one particular Bose headphone model and put a link to the product page on Amazon for people to buy it.

And within a few weeks, I had made my first sale.

I logged into my Amazon Associates account and saw that I had earned $2.18. While that wasn't a lot of money, I was still blown away by the fact that I could actually make free cash online. That experience made affiliate marketing instantly addictive and really fun at the same time. So I created more web pages on that site that reviewed other Bose headphone models as a way to capitalize on the strategies I had put into place to make that first sale.

Over time, I graduated from that free blogging platform and eventually bought my own domain name and signed up for a paid web hosting service. I also dipped into more niches and started making affiliate sites around other things that I was interested in. I was fresh out of college during those days and any free moment I had outside of my regular full-time job I used to work on my affiliate sites. I also joined several SEO forums like Black Hat World, Warrior Forum, and Digital Point and watched as many YouTube videos as I could to find tips and tricks on how to get my sites to rank higher in Google for certain keywords.

What I noticed then, and still do today, is that most people in those forums and on the videos were focused only on the technical aspects of getting to the first page of Google. They openly discussed the importance of site structure and internal linking as well as how to build strong backlinks and manipulate on-page SEO factors to boost your ranking positions. Some people also talked about ways in which you could improve the E-A-T (Expertise, Authority, and Trust) signals of your site to gain favor with Google's algorithm. And while all of those things did help to get my affiliate sites onto page one of Google for their target keywords, those tricks were really only a small part of the equation for being a successful affiliate marketer. Sure, you could have the top ranking page for high traffic buying keywords, but if your content doesn't persuade visitors to click on your affiliate links and make an immediate purchase, then those high ranking positions are not doing you much good.

I learned that lesson the hard way. I had a site that was ranking in the top three positions of Google for some highly competitive keywords; however, that site barely made any money. All of those tricks I had learned on how to snag those top spots in the search engine were pointless because my affiliate pages didn't convert the visitors I was getting into actual buyers. When I looked at the analytics data, many of those pages had high bounce rates as well as low click-through rates and conversions on the products I promoted.

At one point, I even thought about giving up on affiliate marketing altogether because the earnings were so low. The initial excitement from making $2.18 during Ed Dale's *30 Day Challenge* was wearing off. After one full year of hustling hard, I barely cracked $100 per month in affiliate commissions. Plus, all of the stuff that people talked about in those forums and on the videos to boost your affiliate page's keyword rankings seemed like a waste of time when there wasn't very much money to actually be made as a result of it.

But after going back and forth about the idea of quitting, I decided not to give up on affiliate marketing. I really wanted to make a solid living off of my affiliate sites. The dream of making thousands of dollars each month from passive income online was intoxicating. I had already proven to myself that money could be made with a simple—*and free*— blogging site, so I decided to keep working at it.

Over the next few years, I began to dive deeper into the psychology behind what motivates consumers to buy things. I figured that there had to be some disconnect between my top ranking affiliate pages and what visitors actually needed from the content in order to make a sale. I also studied the art of persuasive copywriting. Perhaps I wasn't even using the right words on the page that made people want to purchase things online.

After reading numerous books and articles on consumer psychology and copywriting, I realized that I had been approaching the content on my affiliate pages all wrong. As I made changes to my highest ranking pages based on the information that I discovered, my affiliate earnings went up. Some pages even doubled in sales after just one or two small tweaks. Other pages continued to compound in earnings after every change I made. One page in particular went from earning $0 while ranking #1 for a target keyword to more than $100 in one week after making a few changes to the content.

That experience made me feel like I had finally hit the jackpot. Finally, all of the time and effort I was putting into my affiliate sites was starting to pay off. My income began to steadily grow month after month after applying the tips and tricks I had learned from those consumer psychology and copywriting resources. However, it wasn't an overnight success. It took about seven full years of studying, researching, and applying the methods I was learning to generate a full-time salary as an affiliate marketer. But the financial reward was well worth the wait.

I remember thinking one day about how much I was earning on auto-pilot from my affiliate sites when I took a vacation to Europe in 2015. As I rode on a Gondola through the canals of Venice, Italy, the thought of how much progress I had made in affiliate marketing hit me. I was amazed at how I was actually making more passive income each week from my affiliate sites than the vacation paycheck I was getting from my current employer. It felt surreal to see my affiliate commissions piling up each day during that vacation when I wasn't doing any work at all on my sites!

But things didn't stop there.

Back at home, I kept reading more books, studying other successful websites, and testing my own ideas in order to grow my affiliate earnings even more. Eventually, I discovered—*and mastered*—a core set of concepts that would work on any affiliate site in any niche to make it successful. And when I applied these new methods (i.e. the "secrets" in this book), my affiliate sites went from making a few thousand dollars a month to earning a six-figure income each year.

When I left my full-time job as a Digital Marketing Director for a college in 2019, I had already been making a six-figure income from my side hustle as an affiliate marketer for several years. I also earned that money without having a staff or anyone else helping me create my affiliate sites. I literally built all of the sites myself with free WordPress themes and wrote all of the content on a $400 laptop.

Today, I do hire a few freelance writers to help me scale up the content output because I own multiple sites, but it's not something I have to do. Most of my affiliate sites are on auto-pilot and continue to earn high commissions without me having to touch them.

Which leads me to why I wanted to write this book.

I know that there are people just like me who have been struggling to become successful in affiliate marketing. A lot of you have affiliate sites that are not earning as much money as you had hoped. And others are interested in getting into the affiliate marketing business but are not quite sure how to do it in the most profitable way.

This book is a culmination of more than a decade of time spent researching, analyzing, and testing everything under the sun to boost my earnings as an affiliate marketer.

What I learned during that time is that it doesn't just boil down to fancy SEO tricks to get higher rankings so you can cash in on those clicks. It's actually the content you write and how you structure the page that's crucial for making a significant amount of passive income online.

The truth is that I've built many affiliate sites that use the exact secrets revealed in this book and each of those sites has earned me a lot of money. I hope that after reading this book you'll realize that your dreams of being a successful affiliate marketer are closer than you think. You'll soon discover that the words you use in your writing and how you arrange the content on the page can make a huge impact on your affiliate earnings. And hopefully, you can use those same secrets to turn your part-time side hustle into a full-time business like I have.

HOW IS THIS BOOK DIFFERENT?

By purchasing this book, you've put your trust in me as your mentor. I know that there are hundreds of other books and courses that you could have chosen, and for that reason, I don't want to waste your time. I want you to get a ton of value out of this book so you can start earning more money as an affiliate marketer today.

Here's how this book is different from other books or courses you may have seen or consumed:

Everything You Learn is Timeless

If you've ever bought a book or taken a course in the past on affiliate marketing, then you've probably bought something that worked great when the content was first released. But over time, that information became outdated. This is especially true if the strategies you learned were based on SEO tactics or backlink building strategies—two things that can wipe out any site during a Google algorithm update.

This book, on the other hand, is an evergreen guide that will be just as useful in 10 years from now as it is today. As I mentioned previously, the secrets in this book are based on more than a decade of my own research, analysis, and testing. So you can rest assured that if they've worked for that long of a time, then they'll work for many more years to come. I've only included strategies and concepts that will remain the same regardless of what technology changes.

I Don't Just Teach You the Methods; I Actually Use Them

If there's one thing I've learned about affiliate marketing, it's that there so many "gurus" out there who are trying to sell you a high-priced course that promises to give you the keys to success. However, what often ends up happening after you buy into some of these programs is that you have to invest even more money into their proprietary system to actually get the results. There's usually a monthly service or software tool that you find out about later down the line that's required to make the whole model work.

I've also seen some of these gurus just regurgitating free tips that they found online and packaging them together as their own so called "master course". They don't actually use the strategies they promote on their own sites (if they even have sites at all!) so there's no actual evidence on how well any of their methods work or not.

The difference you'll find between me and those gurus is that I have no hidden agenda. Everything I know and use to boost the earnings on my affiliate sites are revealed in this book.

I didn't just write a book based on theory either. I actually spent years testing various tactics that are based on consumer psychology, persuasive copywriting, and conversion rate optimization. All of the methods that did increase my affiliate earnings I continue to use on every site I own today and any of the things that didn't work were dropped.

Once you learn the affiliate content secrets and page structures that I reveal in this book, you can start implementing them today without having to pay a high price for this proven advice. The only cost for admission is your small investment in this book.

There's no specific route you have to go through either to get the strategies outlined in these pages to work. You can pick and choose which tactics you want to try now to get fast results or make a long-term plan for how you're going to implement all of them to maximum success.

At this point in my affiliate marketing career, I have all of the secrets in this book memorized. So I apply every strategy on every page I publish without having to think about it. My hope for you is that these tactics become ingrained in your own writing workflow and affiliate page structures so that every piece of content you write is as successful as it can be from the start.

HOW TO READ AND APPLY THIS BOOK

This book is structured to work for all types of people. Some of you want to see results fast, and you'll get that with this book. While others like to review an entire process before jumping into things, and that can be achieved too.

You can approach this book in two ways:

1. Read one chapter at a time. Then after each chapter, immediately apply the method you learned to your affiliate pages to see the results.

2. Read through the entire book from beginning to end. Then go back and apply the methods you like best to your affiliate pages. This approach will let you see how everything works before making any adjustments to your existing content.

Regardless of the route you choose for applying the methods learned in this book, the end result is the same: a more effective affiliate site that converts more visitors into buyers. And that's the entire goal with affiliate marketing. The speed at which you get there doesn't necessarily matter because once a good system is put into place, it will continue to deliver rewards for years to come.

I'm really excited for you to dive in and discover how simple it can be to increase the earnings on your affiliate site. I hope you enjoy everything you're about to learn here and get a ton of value out of this book.

So let's get started!

SECTION 1

AFFILIATE WRITING SECRETS

If you want to maximize your earning potential on every affiliate page you publish, then you'll need to use a few tricks of the trade when it comes to writing the content.

In this section, you'll learn my top secrets for how to write affiliate content that's more engaging and persuasive for your visitors. As you'll discover, if you can do a better job at hooking your readers into the page with your words and also convincing them to make a quick buying decision, then you can easily increase your click-through rates and conversions on the affiliate products you promote.

Consider this list of secrets your private playbook to pull from whenever you're writing a new affiliate buying guide or updating an existing page. The affiliate writing secrets that I reveal in this section are the golden nuggets I've uncovered and put together from reading hundreds of books and articles on consumer psychology and persuasive copywriting. What you'll find here are the exact same tips and strategies I've used for years to make my own affiliate sites more profitable. And these methods can work for you too no matter what affiliate program you're using or the niche that your site is in.

If you want to be a more successful affiliate marketer, then you have to be strategic about how you write your content. You can't just publish a generic affiliate buying guide that sounds like it was written by just anyone—*or to anyone*—and expect to maximize your earnings.

IT'S NOT WHAT YOU SAY, IT'S HOW YOU SAY IT

The overall concept that you'll learn in this section is that your affiliate content must contain a strategic blend of two types of writing: copywriting and content writing. And this new way of approaching your affiliate pages has one ultimate goal: to persuade people to act now by clicking on your affiliate links and purchasing the products you recommend without even thinking about going to other websites for additional information.

Now take a moment to let that idea sink in.

Seriously, let it really sink in.

That's a pretty bold statement.

Can it really be possible?

Can you actually persuade more people to click on your affiliate links and to buy more of the products you recommend just by the words you use on the page?

Can you really make your content seem so authoritative that people don't feel like they'll gain anything more by visiting other sites that also talk about the same topic?

The answer to those questions is yes, and you'll soon discover how to do just that by the way you write you write your affiliate content. To quote a common cliché, "It's not what you say, it's how you say it".

Since you're reading this book, I'm going to make a guess that you do mostly "content writing" when you're creating new affiliate articles. Perhaps you've never even heard of the word "copywriting" before or thought that it was basically the same thing as content writing. I want to assure you that it's not.

But for those of you who do know what the difference is between copywriting and content writing, please stay with me because you're just a few paragraphs ahead of your peers in understanding where I'm going with all of this.

As an affiliate marketer, your mission is to get your readers to take a specific action (i.e. buy a product) without going anywhere else to do more research or comparison shop. Essentially, you're trying to influence—*and motivate*—people to make a quick buying decision just by reading the information on your affiliate pages.

And for good reasons too.

If you've been in affiliate marketing for while now, then you know firsthand that if a person doesn't make a purchase before leaving your site, then the next site's affiliate link they click on will get full credit for the commission. And that's the worst thing that can happen for you as an affiliate marketer—lose a sale that you primed the buyer to make.

Therefore, it's crucial that you get as many of your visitors as possible to stick around to read your content and to buy something before they even have a chance to think about going somewhere else. But how do you persuade people to buy the stuff that you're linking to on your affiliate pages without them going to other places to seek out more information?

That, my friend, is where the true power of the affiliate writing secrets I'm about to reveal to you comes into play. In fact, the core principles I outline in this book are what have helped me transform a handful of mediocre affiliate sites into a massive six-figure business. And these writing tips and strategies can do the same thing for you as long as you follow the specific methods as they're laid out.

As I mentioned previously, the overall concept behind writing successful affiliate content is that it must contain a strategic blend of two writing methods: copywriting and content writing. These styles must be interwoven together in a precise way to entice your readers to buy something—*today*—through the links on your affiliate site. To become a master at this affiliate writing method, you have to create a good balance between those two forms of writing. Otherwise, you could be leaving piles of money on the table. But once you do apply these writing strategies the correct way, your affiliate earnings will no longer have a ceiling. That's because your content will be better at meeting your reader's needs and that can translate into higher click-through rates and conversions for the affiliate products you promote.

Now before I wrap this all up and start showing you the affiliate writing secrets that can help to boost your earnings, I want to quickly go over what copywriting is and how it's different from content writing. It's important for you to understand the distinction between these two writing styles and why you need both forms of writing to maximize the earning potential for each affiliate page.

COPYWRITING VS CONTENT WRITING

What is Copywriting?

Simply put, copywriting is a written form of salesmanship. The most common places you'll find this type of persuasive content is in advertisements and publicity materials, such as sales letters and direct mailings.

The goal of good copywriting is to use written words to convince someone to take a particular action, like requesting more information about a product or service, setting up a free consultation so a salesperson can try to close a deal with the interested person, or in our case, to buy an affiliate product that's being reviewed.

For most people, copywriting doesn't come naturally as they write. You have to train yourself on how to use it—and use it well.

As an affiliate marketer, your goal is to harness the persuasive power of copywriting in your content so you can drive more sales for the products you promote.

What is Content Writing?

Content writing is a technical form of writing. There's no sales language in it. The most common places you'll find this type of writing is in instructional and informational content, such as how-to articles and product reviews.

The goal of good content writing is to share information about a topic in a way that educates people on something they want to learn more about. Content writing often includes a lot of technical specifications and details.

If you're actively writing your own affiliate buying guides, then you're likely already doing long forms of content writing. But if you're just starting out in affiliate marketing and haven't written a single product review yet, then you'll quickly become acquainted with this method of writing. That's because it's the most natural way for people to write on affiliate sites.

As an affiliate marketer, content writing is at the core of your business. It's how you educate your readers on the products you're trying to sell. But it can't be the only way you write. Your affiliate content must also have persuasive copywriting used throughout it. Otherwise, you won't convert as many of your casual visitors into active buyers.

WHERE THE REAL MAGIC HAPPENS: BLENDING COPYWRITING WITH CONTENT WRITING

In the pages that follow, you'll discover the exact affiliate writing secrets I use to squeeze every ounce of profit I can out of the people who come to my affiliate sites. What you'll learn next is that when you master the fine art of blending copywriting with content writing, you can essentially write fewer articles and earn more money in the process. When people are interested in and believe what you have to say about a particular topic, they're not going to think about the fact that you're trying to sell them something. Instead, they'll feel like you're the top resource on a subject and hang on your every word. And that subconscious quality can encourage more people to buy the products you recommend through your affiliate links.

When your content speaks to your visitor's desires, addresses their fears, and uses words that they use, it feels more like a conversation with a friend or trusted advisor, and that can disarm them. By putting the right kinds of words in front of your audience, you can make it easier for people to do what you suggest. It's kind of hypnotic, actually.

Now if that sounds like something you want to learn, then turn the page. You'll find 25 secrets in this section that can help you transform your affiliate pages into captivating content that your readers enjoy and pay close attention to.

SECRET #1

IDENTIFY YOUR TARGET BUYER PERSONA

When a lot of us first get into affiliate marketing, we don't really think about it as a business. Instead, we just look at it as a way to make some quick and easy money online. Some of also believe that all we have to do is write some decent product reviews with our affiliate links attached and then get those pages to rank high in Google. By doing this, we can then cash in on the visitors who happen to buy the stuff we recommend.

In the beginning of my affiliate marketing career, I approached my own affiliate sites in that same way. And while that process did work to make some money, it wasn't anything to brag about. It was actually when I changed my mindset and began treating my affiliate sites like they were real businesses that my earnings started to skyrocket.

I remember one site in particular that had a decent amount of earnings from every page that I tossed up on it. I would literally crank out an affiliate buying guide in a couple of hours and it would earn anywhere from $25 to $50 per month. And because that process was working, I never questioned it. I would just rinse and repeat what I was doing and post new affiliate buying guides using the same basic content writing tactics.

But as I grew the number of sites that I managed, I had to force myself to look at this affiliate marketing game as an actual business. I had to find ways to streamline my workflows and squeeze additional profit out of each piece of affiliate content I published.

The reason I got so serious about turning my affiliate side hustle into an actual business was because I wanted to quit working for someone else and become a self-employed affiliate marketer—a dream that I hope you can also achieve by reading this book.

Essentially, what I realized back then was that I couldn't just write for fun anymore and hope to make some good money at it. I had to have an actual content writing plan that would work to achieve that goal. And the success of that plan ended up hinging on targeting certain types of buyers for every affiliate page I wrote.

BUYER PERSONAS ARE A STRATEGIC STARTING POINT

After months of reading various business books and talking to other entrepreneurs on how I could improve my affiliate business, I discovered the important concept of buyer personas. I had stumbled across this idea in the past but I overlooked it because it was always referenced in the scope of selling products and services as a *real business* that was meeting a specific need in the marketplace. I never once came across anyone in the online marketing groups I participated in mentioning the use of buyer personas in affiliate marketing. The people on those sites just talked about the latest SEO tricks that could be used to rank higher in Google since that seemed to be the most important goal for an affiliate site.

By talking to entrepreneurs in other industries, I got to thinking, "If this strategic business concept of using buyer personas was so powerful for real businesses, then why couldn't I use it to improve my own affiliate sites?" Since I was actively trying to transform my collection of affiliate sites into a full-time business, I figured I would give it a try.

And when I did, the results were astounding.

The affiliate content that I wrote based on buyer personas earned so much more money than the content I had thrown up on my sites without using that strategy. It was as if I had found a hidden barrel of rocket fuel that I could use to propel any one of my affiliate page's earnings. And it wasn't that hard to take advantage of the income-boosting power of buyer personas either. All that was required was a simple shift in the way I approached my affiliate content writing from the start.

WHAT IS A BUYER PERSONA?

In business, the buyer persona is a fictitious representation of your ideal target customer. In other words, it's the specific kind of person who you think would most likely buy your stuff.

Buyer personas help all of us who are in any form of marketing or sales because they help us internalize the ideal customer we're trying to attract and persuade to buy our products and services. Having a deep understanding of buyer personas is critical for any business that wants to be successful in its product development, content creation, customer acquisition, and retention. And they can work wonders for you as an affiliate marketer too.

Whenever you write a new piece of affiliate content, you should always start by coming up with a target buyer persona for that page. That way, you know exactly who you're writing the content for and can meet that person's every need. This step is important to begin with because when people are choosing who to trust, they naturally gravitate toward others who show a genuine understanding and concern for them. And gaining that trust requires a subtle, but very important, shift in how you present yourself through the words in your affiliate content.

The best piece of advice I can give you here before we get into the rest of this book is to never lay a finger on your keyboard until you first decide who you're targeting with your affiliate content. If you don't start with the *who* then you won't know how to write the most effective content. There's also a strong likelihood that you won't convert as many of your casual readers into active buyers.

I hope your goal for reading this book is to become a master affiliate marketer—one that does everything they can to create the highest earning potential for every page they publish. If that's what you want out of your affiliate sites, then don't skip this important first step of creating your target buyer persona for every page you create. It's a simple, yet powerful tactic you can use to make your content more relatable and convincing for your audience.

HOW DO YOU CREATE A BUYER PERSONA?

Creating a buyer persona is a lot easier than you may think. All you have to do is visualize the person who you're writing the content for by asking yourself these types of questions:

- What does this person look like?
- How old are they?
- What's their job title?
- What challenges do they face?
- What are their dreams and aspirations?
- Are they a mom or dad or a teenager?
- Do they talk a certain way?
- Are they offended by foul language or do they use it?
- What does their day look like?
- How do they make buying decisions?

This list of questions could go on and on, but the ultimate goal is for you to picture the perfect customer who you think would buy the products you're trying to sell on an affiliate page. Then write down the attributes you think that person has.

There's no right or wrong answer here either. Just go with your instincts.

Once you have your buyer persona created, you can start targeting that person with your affiliate content. Focusing on this step up front can help you earn more money as an affiliate marketer because the person who reads your article and matches those characteristics will think that you're writing directly to them, which is how you want them to feel.

The more a reader feels like you understand them, the easier it is for them to trust you and follow your recommendations on which products to buy. And that's the whole purpose of writing affiliate content in the first place, isn't it?

AN EXAMPLE USING A BUYER PERSONA

We'll now look at an example of a target buyer persona and some sample affiliate content that has been written to appeal to that type of person. This will help you to see how this affiliate writing secret actually works.

For this example, we'll imagine that we're writing the following affiliate buying guide, *Top 10 Best Video Baby Monitors*. And the attributes of the person who comes to mind that would likely buy these types of products include:

- New mother
- Caucasian
- Between 22 to 34 years of age
- Middle-class
- Enjoys her freedom
- Concerned about safety
- Uses trendy words
- Dresses in the latest fashions
- Has a good salary
- Doesn't have a lot of free time to spare
- Loves to find a bargain

With those traits in mind, we can custom tailor the language on our affiliate buying guide to meet this type of person's personality and expectations.

If I were to write the *Top 10 Best Video Baby Monitors* guide based on the above target buyer persona, then I would use phrases like these below throughout the content:

- Are you a new mama (or "mum" as they say in the UK)?
- Don't worry if you're a total noob. Thousands of other new mothers are in the same boat as you. In fact, about 360,000 new bundles of joy are born each day! Crazy to think, huh? Have you ever wondered where all of those dirty diapers go? Eek! Anyways, I digress. Let's keep moving on so you can find the best video baby monitor for your needs.

Phrases Continued...

- No matter if you're 22 or 34, a video baby monitor is one of the best investments you can make as a new mommy.
- These products give you the peace of mind you need to ensure that your baby is super-safe and totally secure, while also giving you that much needed free time to get other important things done around the house.
- If you're looking for a good deal (which is why we wrote this guide in the first place!), then you're going to love this first product recommendation. It has everything—*and I mean everything*—you'd ever want in a video baby monitor.

Now contrast that type of language with these phrases below that are not based on a target buyer persona.

- Are you a new parent?
- Being a new parent should not cause you so much worry. Thousands of men and women are going through this same experience right now. Statistically, 360,000 new infants are born each day.
- Video baby monitors are good for any parent.
- These products offer enhanced safety and security for your baby. They also give you the chance to do other things around the house without being interrupted.
- Here is my first recommendation. I hope it has all of the features you or your spouse is looking for in a video baby monitor.

What did you think after reading the first set of phrases with the language that was targeting a specific buyer persona? Didn't you feel like it really hit the mark for new mothers who might be reading that content for the first time?

I hope you agree that new moms would instantly connect with that type of language on an affiliate buying guide for video baby monitors because it's more relatable and makes them feel understood. On a subconscious level, the words that were used in those phrases would make most mothers who fit within that target buyer persona's characteristics more comfortable taking the product recommendations on that affiliate page.

The second set of phrases had language that was too generic. It was bland, boring, and not focused on the needs of one particular type of person. As you read the content, didn't it seem like it was trying to appeal to everyone who might land on the page (i.e. moms, dads, old, and young)? Writing like that is not as effective for affiliate content that you want to convert at the highest rate. If a new mom came across a video baby monitor buying guide that had phrases written like that, she would probably leave before ever clicking on an affiliate link. The content just doesn't resonate as well with that type of buyer or give her any reason to stick around to consider the product recommendations seriously.

As you can see, creating buyer personas for the type of person who is most likely to land on your affiliate pages is essential for keeping your writing centered on their needs. Just writing for writing sake, or just using language without any care for how it comes across, is not the best course of action when you're trying to make the most money on every affiliate page you publish.

If you want to be a more successful affiliate marketer, then you should tailor each piece of content you write so it speaks directly to a target buyer persona. Doing that can help to maximize your affiliate earnings on any page. And you don't have to limit yourself to only using this writing secret on new content either. In fact, you can get started on creating your first buyer persona today by looking at one of your existing affiliate articles and thinking about who that content is best suited for. Then, ask yourself the types of questions that were referenced earlier in this chapter to narrow down the characteristics of that target buyer persona. Finally, edit the page and change the wording so it speaks more directly to that kind of person. Use the language that you think they would use and mention the things that you believe would interest them the most.

By rewriting your existing affiliate pages with a target buyer persona in mind, you can instantly see the results of your work by tracking the changes in the click-through rates and conversions of the affiliate products you promote. If those metrics go up, then you know that you're targeting the right buyer persona with that content.

BUT WON'T THIS TACTIC ALIENATE MY OTHER VISITORS?

This is a common fear that people have when they first hear about using buyer personas to craft their content. I had the same concern myself, so I know firsthand just how scary it can be to write new articles with this type of intent and to rewrite existing affiliate buying guides that are generating a decent amount of income. But I can tell you that after I pushed through those fears and tried it, I had much more success.

The truth is that when you focus your writing through buyer personas, then you can actually experience an increase in your affiliate sales. The reason this happens is because more of the right kind of people are engaged with and persuaded by your content. When it comes to marketing in general, you can't please everyone. And the faster you realize this, the more money you can make from your affiliate site. With each affiliate page you create, your main goal should be to meet the needs of a particular type of person who is ready to make an immediate purchase. And if you can make your content seem more relatable to those kinds of people, then you can experience higher click-through rates and conversions for the products you promote than trying to appeal to every single visitor who lands on your page.

SECRET #2

ACT LIKE AN AUTHORITY

If you're anything like me, then you try to stay up to date on the latest SEO news and online marketing tips that come out each week. As affiliate marketers, we have to keep our eyes peeled for the next-best thing that can help us improve our sites. Like with any online business, you have to constantly be learning and growing in your skills in order to remain successful.

What I find interesting about the SEO and affiliate marketing world in this regard is that there are so many self-proclaimed masters who seem to possess all of the *secrets* when it comes to making bucketloads of money online. It's as if these mini celebrities (or influencers) have some magical source that provides them with the hidden insights for major success that no one else can tap into. And so many of us affiliate marketers hang on their every word for practical advice.

We listen intently to everything these have to say in hopes of scooping up any free golden nuggets of information they drop along the way. But the really good stuff often only comes with a price. You have to buy their expensive course or pay a high cost for a personal consultation to get their expert advice. And many of us are willing to do those things because these influencers seem so knowledgeable. Also, we feel the pressure to get unstuck and move forward with making our affiliate sites more profitable. Therefore, we feel like any investment we make to achieve that dream is worth it.

But this type of thing doesn't just happen in the marketing world. It happens everywhere. People follow influencers of every kind, in every niche, including fitness, nutrition, home and garden, sports, health, politics, money, etc. No space is immune to influencers. However, if you examine these influencers closely, you'll find that all of these mini celebrities have one thing in common: they predominantly use 1st person singular pronouns in their messaging (*more on that in a bit*). That's why so many of us look up to these people as authorities in their niches. These influencers seem to know firsthand so much more than the rest of us because they have a deeper level of knowledge on everything they talk about. And we, as their audience, are eager to get a taste of anything they're willing to share.

We all fall prey to this too. I'm definitely guilty of it. But it's often more pronounced in certain areas of our lives more than others. Most commonly, we look to influencers (i.e. authorities) for advice when we have a strong passion about something but we don't have the expert knowledge on the topic. In these situations, we tend to seek out others who already have the expertise in a particular area to tell us what to do and what to think. It's a natural instinct for us to act this way too. Internally, we all want to avert pain in the fastest way possible. That's why we latch onto the thoughts and opinions of these self-proclaimed authorities in the various niches they represent. By accepting what they proclaim as the truth, we can quickly sweep away our doubts and confusion on a subject and feel like we're getting the answers we've been seeking.

The fact is that it's nearly impossible to be an expert in everything, so we have to let others lead us in some areas of our lives. Otherwise, we wouldn't be able to learn as much as we'd like to or get as much done. It's kind of like when you were in school. When you were growing up, you depended on the information that was being taught to you by others. And that knowledge is what helped you get to where you are today.

IT'S EASIER TO SELL THINGS WHEN YOU'RE THE AUTHORITY

Now you may have never thought about the idea of becoming a top authority in your affiliate niche before. But if you do, you can radically increase your click-through rates and conversions of the products you promote on your affiliate pages. When it comes to affiliate content writing, your opinion does count. And to some people, it counts a lot.

So much so, that they'll buy anything you recommend just because you seem like the top authority on the subject.

Let me give you a quick example of what I mean.

Suppose you're writing an affiliate buying guide on *The Best Guitars for Left-Handed People*. When someone lands on your page, chances are that they need some serious help picking a good guitar as a left-handed person. If they didn't, they wouldn't be reading your content in the first place.

Now imagine how that person would feel if they read something on your buying guide that was along these lines:

> "As a lefty myself, I personally know how hard it can be to find a good guitar for people like us. In fact, I spent about three weeks sifting through hundreds of reviews on left-handed guitars to find the select few that actually work well—*and sound good*—in a right-handed world. On this page, I'll show what I found and explain why I like each guitar so much. I'll also point out which one I chose for myself and the top features it has. I hope you find the best left-handed guitar for your needs in the list of reviews below."

If a left-handed person read that text above, they would instantly feel like they're on a web page where the person who wrote it has a high level of knowledge and authority on the subject of left-handed guitars. As a way to be more persuasive, we revealed that you were lefty yourself and went through the same struggles as the reader to find a good left-handed guitar. Therefore, you clearly know what you're talking about on the subject. And many left-handed guitarists who read content written like that would probably take your advice for which guitars to consider because you seem so authoritative on the topic.

But what's really going on behind the scenes here that makes this language so powerful, authoritative, and persuasive is that it uses 1st person singular pronouns. And this is a secret writing trick you can use in your own affiliate content to make it just as good.

WHAT IS A 1ST PERSON SINGULAR PRONOUN?

First-person singular pronouns are the words "I", "me", "my", and "mine". These are words that you use in writing when you're referring to yourself. And they can be very persuasive when you're trying to convince someone to buy something on your affiliate pages.

Consider the statement I made earlier in this chapter, "The fact is that it's nearly impossible to be an expert in everything, so we have to let others lead us in some areas of our lives." When it comes to people searching for individual product reviews and recommendations on the best choices in a particular category, that argument gets proven over and over again. And the affiliate sites that position themselves as the top authorities for those categories are the ones who usually make the most money.

Using 1st person singular pronouns like "I", "me", "my", and "mine" in your affiliate content can give the perception that your page has more authority and expertise on a subject, which can help drive more sales for the products you promote.

Now I know that not everyone who reads this chapter can follow this content writing secret to the letter. That's because some of you don't make your affiliate articles look like they're coming from a single author. And others of you may not have the privilege of using 1st person singular pronouns in your writing because you're working on behalf of a company and must use a certain type of voice in the content. If that's you, then don't worry, because the next two secrets (#3 and #4) will be more than enough to meet your needs.

However, if you can adjust the content on your affiliate site so that it's coming from a single person or several individual authors who can establish themselves as the experts on certain subjects, then you should definitely do it. Writing in the 1st person is a subtle and very effective way to add authoritativeness to every piece of affiliate content you publish.

HOW TO USE 1ST PERSON SINGULAR PRONOUNS

We'll now look at some examples of 1st person singular pronouns so you can see exactly how this writing method works. In the list below, I've underlined the 1st person singular pronouns in each sentence so they're easy to pick out. Use these examples to help generate your own ideas on how to use this type of writing in your affiliate content.

- I want you to get the best deal for your money, so I put together this detailed guide on the top portable shavers for men. Every single shaver on this list is one that I would use personally to shave my beard. And I'm very picky about what touches my beard.

- A lot of people ask me, "James, what would you pick? Do you like the John Deere or Cub Cadet tractor the most?" What I tell those people is that when I'm trying to cut my yard as fast as possible so I can move on to more important things, like watching the latest NASCAR race, I need my tractor to have the best steering, turning, and stability possible. Therefore, the John Deere tractor is my go-to tractor every time.

- The thing I like most about this hair conditioner is the plant-based oils. I have pretty thick hair and the strategic blend of plant-based oils really works to soften up my hair follicles. Nothing else I have ever tried has worked so well with my thick hair. If you're like me, then this may be the best hair conditioner for you too.

- You might find the trigger on this pellet gun to be a little sensitive as it was with mine. But after a bit of practice, you'll get used to it. I sure did, and now I love the speed at which I can fire off round after round at my targets.

- If you're having a hard time losing weight, then I suggest that you try this program here. I also struggled with my weight and I found this program to be the easiest one to follow—*and stick with*—to lose those extra pounds. I can't recommend it enough to people who want to lose a lot of weight fast.

After reading those examples, you can hopefully see the power behind using 1st person singular pronouns in your affiliate content. By putting your personal opinions and firsthand experiences at the forefront of your content, you can give your readers a strong sense of your authority on a subject. And with the recent rise in popularity of influencers online, you'll fit right in with the crowd when writing this way. So go ahead and try to incorporate the use of 1st person singular pronouns in your affiliate content and see for yourself just how much more convincing it can be for your readers.

With that said, I'd like to end this chapter with these parting words of advice, "Don't go too overboard with this writing tactic by *only* using the words 'I', 'me', 'my', and 'mine' on your affiliate pages." If you only write in the 1st person, then you won't make a deep connection with your readers. Sure, you may impress them with your expertise and knowledge, but they may not feel like you're talking directly to them in order to help them solve their problems. A better approach is to add in a strategic blend of 2nd person pronouns to make your content even more appealing to your audience, which I'll cover in the next chapter.

SECRET #3

WRITE DIRECTLY TO YOUR READERS

How would you like to submerge your readers directly into the narrative of your affiliate content? If you could tell your audience what to believe, feel, and how to react, how much easier do you think it would be for you to convince them to buy the products you recommend?

Engaging your readers in a richer sensory experience; where they can see, smell, hear, taste, or touch something; is one of the best ways to persuade people with your writing. When a person feels like you're writing directly to them, they feel much closer to you and the ideas that you present.

It's no wonder why so many of the most popular self-help books are written in the perspective of the second-person. Writing from the point of view of talking to the reader puts that person in the central role of the content and allows the writer to include them within the narrative. That's why many of us come away from reading a self-help book with immediate thoughts like, "I can do this!" and "I can make the change!"

You can achieve a similar effect with your own affiliate content through the use of 2nd person pronouns by making people think, "This is the right product for me!", which can help lead to an increase in affiliate sales. This chapter will teach you how to do just that.

WHAT IS A 2ND PERSON PRONOUN?

Second-person pronouns are the words "you" and "your". These are words you use in writing when you're addressing the person who is reading the content. And those two simple words ("you" and "your") can be very persuasive. In fact, they're the next best thing to using your reader's actual name throughout the page.

The advantage of using 2nd person pronouns is that they help your readers quickly connect the points in your copy to their own lives. When a reader sees the words "you" and "your", they're subconsciously drawn into the text and feel like the content was written personally for them. An immediate feeling of being involved occurs.

To show you how this writing technique works, take a look at the following two examples. Then, ask yourself which one (A or B) do you find to be the most compelling.

- **A:** This product has five different colors choices and comes in two sizes: large and small.
- **B:** You get five different color choices with this product and you can choose between two sizes: large and small.

After reading those two sentences, you hopefully picked example B as being the most compelling version.

What makes example B much more engaging is that it speaks directly to the reader and draws them into the content by using the word "you". Second-person pronouns like this have a hypnotic power over the audience because these words are self-referencing language. This pronoun form enhances the relevance of the subject matter that you're referring to in your content, and therefore, agitates the benefit or problem more effectively.

USE 2ND PERSON PRONOUNS AND MUCH AS YOU CAN

While 2nd person pronouns may be little words, they have a major impact on how people respond to your affiliate content. So you should use them as much as you can in your writing. It's also a good idea to intersperse 2nd person pronouns along with 1st person singular pronouns like I mentioned in the last chapter. That way you can establish authority on a topic by sharing your firsthand experiences and knowledge while also immersing your readers into the narrative.

One of the best ways to take advantage of this content writing secret is to first look through your existing affiliate pages with a fresh set of eyes. Next, take note of the sentences on those pages that don't sound personal to the reader. Then, rewrite that content so it speaks more directly to your audience. If you follow my advice in *Secret #1* about creating a unique target buyer persona for each of your affiliate pages, then it should be easy for you to come up with the right type of language that appeals to your readers.

Try to update as many sentences as you can on your affiliate pages too. Go ahead and litter your content with the 2nd person pronouns "you" and "your" without worrying about it being overkill. By using 2nd person pronouns, your content will connect much better with your readers and help them feel more comfortable taking your advice on which products to buy. In turn, that can lead to an increase in your affiliate earnings.

HOW TO USE 2ND PERSON PRONOUNS

We'll now look at some examples of 2nd person pronouns so you can see exactly how this writing method works. That way you can get the juices flowing for how to transform your own affiliate content into something that's much more direct and inclusive.

Next, you'll see several sets of two sentences. The first sentence is the original text without the use of 2nd person pronouns. The second sentence has been modified to include this pronoun form. I've underlined the 2nd person pronouns in each of the modified sentences so you can pick them out easily.

Original: It's a nice product for the money.
Modified: You won't find anything else like it for your money.

Original: There's a 5-year limited warranty on this device.
Modified: You get a 5-year limited warranty with this device. Not only does that protect your investment, but it also saves you money in the long-run on costly repairs.

Examples Continued...

Original: How does that feature relate to better game play?
Modified: How can you get better game play with this feature?

Original: This 7-stage air cleaning system is one-of-a-kind.
Modified: You'll be blown away by the 7-stage air cleaning system. If you want something that's one-of-a-kind, then this is your top choice.

Original: One thing that this machine is missing is a remote control. But the other products on this page do have that feature.
Modified: If you care about having the convenience of a remote control, then you'll want to check out one of the other machines on this page. They'll suit your needs much better.

After reading those examples, you can hopefully see how easy it is to transform a non-personal sentence into one that's more inclusive for the reader just by using 2nd person pronouns. You also should have come away with the feeling that the modified sentences were much more persuasive for the audience. By including the words "you" and "your", those examples were able to draw the reader in and tell them how they should feel, think, and react.

I encourage you to go through and update your existing affiliate pages with 2nd person pronouns and to also start incorporating this type of writing in your new content. With this approach, you should see higher engagement rates on your affiliate pages by having longer pageview times and lower bounce rates. After you're done modifying your affiliate pages to include 2nd person pronouns, you'll then want to consider using 1st person plural pronouns that I cover in the next chapter. By combining 2nd person pronouns with 1st person plural pronouns, as well as 1st person singular pronouns mentioned in *Secret #2*, you can instantly change your affiliate content from being flat and lifeless into something that's highly engaging and persuasive.

SECRET #4

BOND WITH YOUR AUDIENCE

If secrets #2 and #3 got you excited about rewriting your affiliate content so it's more appealing to your readers, then this chapter is going to be the icing on the cake. What's nice about the secret that I'll discuss here is that you can use this writing technique regardless if your affiliate pages are written by a single author or from a collective voice as is commonplace on an organization's site.

By following the advice I have for you in this chapter about writing with 1st person plural pronouns, you can instantly create a bond with your audience. And that connection can make the act of persuading someone to buy the products you recommend much easier on an affiliate site.

WHAT IS A 1ST PERSON PLURAL PRONOUN?

First-person plural pronouns are the words "we", "us", and "our", and these words can be used in two ways in your writing. The first way is the traditional method by using 1st person plural pronouns to refer to the group that's writing the content. For example, you might find something like this on a corporate site, "We have been in business for 25 years." Or you might come across a statement like this on a company blog, "Our technical team spent three weeks analyzing the data for this latest article."

We won't be discussing the traditional method of using 1st person plural pronouns in this chapter because it doesn't necessarily help us make our affiliate content more persuasive. Instead, we'll be focusing on the second way that you can use this pronoun form in your writing which is to create a bond with your readers. For example, you may find something like this on an affiliate buying guide, "People like us often want a money-back guarantee on our purchases and this product gives us that peace of mind." Or something along these lines, "I want all of us to get the best product for our computers. As new interior designers, we can't afford to waste billable hours working with a clunky piece of software".

The advantage of writing with 1st person plural pronouns is that you can trigger a subconscious response in your audience. When you use words like "we", "us", and "our", you're essentially bringing the reader into the emotional context of your statements and transferring your thoughts and opinions onto them. And when people read statements that include 1st person plural pronouns that are used in a strategic way, those individuals can be persuaded more easily to agree with what you have to say and to take a specific type of action, such as purchasing one of your product recommendations.

HOW TO USE 1ST PERSON PLURAL PRONOUNS

We'll now look at some examples of 1st person plural pronouns so you can see exactly how this writing method works. That way you can start coming up with your own ideas on how to incorporate this writing form into your affiliate content.

Next, you'll see several sets of two sentences. The first sentence is the original text without the use of 1st person plural pronouns. The second sentence has been modified to include this pronoun form. I've underlined the 1st person plural pronouns in each of the modified sentences so you can pick them out easily.

Original: People typically want more features for their money, but this espresso machine gives them the best warranty.
Modified: We typically want more features for our money, but this espresso machine gives us the best warranty.

Examples Continued...

Original: Some people agree that this pair of boxing gloves meets all of the basic needs for a beginner boxer.
Modified: I think we can all agree that this pair of boxing gloves meets our basic needs as beginner boxers.

Original: Can I tell you about the best part of this robot vacuum really quick? Like how insanely clean a living room can get with the room mapping feature?
Modified: Can we talk about the best part of this robot vacuum really quick? Like how insanely clean our living rooms can get with the room mapping feature?

Original: That's the most important thing a hunter needs—a good pair of insulated hunting boots so they don't freeze their toes off in the woods.
Modified: That's the most important thing hunters like us need—a good pair of insulated hunting boots so we don't freeze our toes off in the woods.

After reading those examples, you can hopefully see how using 1st person plural pronouns can make the reader feel more united with the person who wrote the content. With just a few simple modifications in word usage to include this pronoun form, your thoughts can subtly become the audience's thoughts as they're reading through your affiliate content.

My final advice for you here is to go through and update your existing affiliate pages with 1st person plural pronouns where you can fit them in. Also, start incorporating this type of writing in your new content. Once I began using this pronoun form on my own affiliate pages, I saw an uptick in my affiliate sales. It was fascinating to witness how one simple change in how I addressed my readers could have such a big impact on my earnings. Hopefully, those same results can happen for you too.

SECRET #5

CHOOSE ACTIVE VOICE OVER PASSIVE VOICE

There are two types of grammatical voices in English grammar called "active voice" and "passive voice". The active voice is the preferred method for writing because it creates a faster-moving narrative that makes your content more engaging to read. It also uses fewer words to get the point across as compared to the passive voice. By using the active voice in your affiliate content, your sentences will be easier to understand and less wordy. The passive voice is a weaker way of writing that can make your content harder to grasp and take more time for your audience to read.

When you're trying to persuade a person to take an action on an affiliate site (i.e. buy a product), it pays dividends to keep your sentences short, clear, and concise by using the active voice. If you use language that's long-winded or confusing, then your content won't be as convincing to your readers. And that can lead to fewer affiliate sales.

Therefore, it's best to get into the habit of writing as many of your sentences as possible in the active voice, which you'll learn in this chapter.

HOW IS AN ACTIVE VOICE SENTENCE STRUCTURED?

Writing in the active voice means that the subject of the sentence acts upon its verb.

You can also think of it this way:

Active Voice = Subject + Verb + Object

HOW IS A PASSIVE VOICE SENTENCE STRUCTURED?

Writing in the passive voice means that the subject of the sentence is the recipient of the verb's action.

You can also think of it this way:

Passive Voice = Object + Verb + Subject

ACTIVE VOICE VERSUS PASSIVE VOICE COMPARED

We'll now compare two sets of sentences to help you better understand the difference between the active voice and passive voice in writing. In the examples below, I underlined the subject, italicized the verb, and bolded the object in each sentence so you can see how they're arranged differently in each type of voice.

Active Voice: The best lawn mower *has* a **30 hp engine**.
Passive Voice: A **30 hp engine** can *be found* on the best lawn mower.

Active Voice: You can *read* this **book** in one day.
Passive Voice: This **book** can be *read* by you in one day.

As you can see from those examples, the active voice sentences are shorter, more concise, and easier to understand. Because the subject acted upon its verb there is no ambiguity when you read the active voice sentences.

In the first set of sentences, the passive voice example is a little convoluted and not very convincing. The sentence says that a 30 hp engine can be found on the best lawn mower. But is a 30 hp engine always on the best model? The passive voice leaves you questioning that statement.

With the active voice sentence there is no confusion. The best lawn mower *has* a 30 hp engine as it has been stated. Period.

In the second set of sentences, you'll find similar things to be true as the first set. The passive voice example says that the book can be read by you in one day. But is that a fact? Or is it just a possibility? When you read that sentence there's still some doubt left in your mind because of the way it has been structured.

But with the active voice sentence, there is no question about whether you can read the book in one day or not. The sentence states it plain and clear: you *can* read this book in one day.

MORE EXAMPLES OF ACTIVE VOICE VERSUS PASSIVE VOICE

For some people, the active voice versus passive voice in writing can be a hard concept to grasp. I know this because it took a while for me to fully understand it too. One thing that did help to make it more clear was seeing more examples of active voice versus passive voice in writing and trying to pick out the subject, verb, and object in each sentence as I read them. So I've repeated that same type of lesson here for you. As you read the sets of sentences below, see if you can pick out the subject, verb, and object in each example so you can get a better understanding of how each type of voice is structured. The answers are revealed on the next page.

Active Voice: The top musicians pick this guitar.
Passive Voice: This guitar is picked by the top musicians.

Active Voice: You don't have to cut carbs on this diet plan.
Passive Voice: This diet plan doesn't require you to cut carbs.

Active Voice: Most people buy two sets of these earrings.
Passive Voice: These earrings are bought in two sets by most people.

Active Voice: You can get free shipping if you order today.
Passive Voice: Free shipping is available if you order today.

Active Voice: Vegetarians prefer these supplements over other brands.
Passive Voice: These supplements are preferred by vegetarians over other brands.

ANSWERS:

The subject is underlined, the verb is italicized, and the object is bolded.

Active Voice: The top musicians *pick* this **guitar**.
Passive Voice: This **guitar** is *picked* by the top musicians.

Active Voice: You don't have to *cut carbs* on this **diet plan**.
Passive Voice: This **diet plan** doesn't require *cutting carbs* for you.

Active Voice: Most people *buy* two sets of these **earrings**.
Passive Voice: These **earrings** are *bought* in two sets by most people.

Active Voice: You can *get* **free shipping** if you order today.
Passive Voice: **Free shipping** is *available* if you order today.

Active Voice: Vegetarians *prefer* these **supplements** over other brands.
Passive Voice: These **supplements** are *preferred* by vegetarians over other brands.

THE ACTIVE VOICE IS MORE PERSUASIVE

The major takeaway for this chapter is that you should try to write all of your affiliate content in the active voice. The only exception to this rule is if you can't write a sentence in any other way. Then, and only then, is the passive voice acceptable in affiliate content that's intended to convert more readers into buyers.

By writing too many sentences in the passive voice, you're likely to confuse your audience and cause doubt in their minds as they're reading your affiliate page. And that can have a negative impact on your click-through rates and conversions. If you want your affiliate content to be as engaging and persuasive as possible, then you need to keep your sentences short, clear, and concise by writing in the active voice.

SECRET #6

USE POWER WORDS

Did you know that you can use certain words to trigger a psychological or emotional response in your readers?

It's true.

In fact, there are some words that are so powerful that you can instantly get people to trust everything that you say. Plus, they're so easy to use. And I can prove it to you. Guaranteed!

The words that I'm referring to here are called "power words" and I just used six of them in that previous paragraph. Do you think you can pick them out? If not, you soon will be after you finish this chapter.

POWER WORDS HEIGHTEN PEOPLE'S AROUSAL

If you're like most people who read that sample paragraph, then you couldn't wait to find out what those powerful words were that I was referring to. That paragraph was written in a way to grab your interest and entice you to want to discover the answer by using a handful of select words. What's great about power words is that they can heighten a reader's arousal and have a highly persuasive quality that's hard for people to resist. You can literally hype up anything you want and bring people to the edge of their seats about any aspect of an affiliate product by using these special types of words. By sprinkling a few power words throughout your affiliate content, you can easily increase your click-through rates because people will feel compelled to find out more about the products you're promoting.

EXAMPLES OF POWER WORDS

So what are these power words that seem to have such a persuasive quality? Below is a list of the top power words you can start using in your affiliate content today.

- Trust
- Guarantee
- Proven
- Results
- Discover
- Easy
- Simple
- Powerful
- Best
- Best-in-class
- Top
- Free
- Bonus
- Exclusive
- Extra
- Save
- Savings
- Deal
- First
- New
- Now
- Today
- Instantly
- Latest
- Win
- Profit

Power Words Continued…

- Safety
- Protect
- Help
- Amazing
- Extraordinary
- Exceptional
- One-of-a-kind
- Ultimate
- Complete

By using any combination of these power words in your affiliate content, you can make your products seem more irresistible to your readers. And once you do that, your audience won't be able to resist taking the next steps to find out more about those offers.

HOW TO USE POWER WORDS

We'll now look at the use of power words in action. Below you'll find some example sentences that include power words. Use these examples to help you generate your own ideas for how to use power words in your affiliate content. I underlined the power words in each sentence so you can pick them out easily.

- This bow hunting knife is <u>one-of-kind</u>. It has an <u>exceptional</u> drop-point blade.
- If you're looking for the <u>ultimate</u> baby stroller, then this is it. This model collapses <u>instantly</u> with the touch of a button so you can <u>easily</u> transfer it to and from the trunk of your car.
- The most <u>amazing</u> quality of this cookware set is the stainless steel material. It's long-lasting, a classic style, and the <u>top</u> choice for browning and braising meats and poultry.
- With this protection plan, you can <u>trust</u> that your home appliances will be covered. It offers <u>best-in-class</u> coverage for every model out there.

Examples Continued...

- You should check out this wireless thermostat now. Last time I looked, there was a <u>fantastic</u> <u>deal</u> with <u>free</u> shipping. Hopefully, you can still grab those same <u>savings</u>.
- This air conditioner is so <u>easy</u> to use that even my 72 year old grandmother could figure it out. And she hates <u>new</u> technology!

As you can see, by adding a few power words into each sentence, the products took on a whole new level of attraction. For example, when someone reads that a product is *one-of-a-kind* or the *ultimate choice*, they can't help but be intrigued to learn more about it. Plus, if something is a *fantastic deal* or *easy to use*, then why not give it a try?

Once you start using power words in your own affiliate content, you'll quickly see just how mighty they can be for your earnings. The more you can make a product sound impressive, the more people will want to check it out and buy it.

What surprises me is that many of the top ranking affiliate pages out there don't include power words at all. My suspicion is that a lot of these writers think that power words sound too salesy and that they'll turn the reader off by using them. However, that's not the case in my experience. From my own personal testing, the pages that include power words earn more money than the pages that don't have them. As you discovered in this secret, power words boost the attraction and desire for a particular product when those words are used well.

So I encourage you to start using power words throughout your own affiliate pages and see for yourself just how much these simple words can improve your product click-through rates and conversions.

SECRET #7

WRITE LIKE A 7TH GRADER (OR EVEN A 3RD GRADER)

The title of this chapter may come as a surprise, but I assure you that this is one of the best content writing secrets for any affiliate marketer. The top business writing schools even teach it to their students. And if you use the writing techniques that I'm about to reveal here, then you can easily make more sales from the products you promote on your affiliate pages.

This powerful writing secret can be summed up in six simple words: *Write to express, not to impress.*

While long-winded sentences with a lot of technical jargon and words pulled from the thesaurus might seem authoritative and intellectual while you're writing them, they're actually harder for most people to comprehend. And confusion is one of the top killers for both click-through rates and conversions on an affiliate site.

When you're writing affiliate content, you want your writing to be lean, clean, and easy to read. So much so that your content is at a 7th grade reading level. Better yet, at a 3rd grade reading level if you can do it. The reason you want to target those lower reading levels is that you'll connect with a wider audience. The average American adult reading level is that of a 9th grader. But studies show that adults prefer reading at least two grades below their ability. It's no wonder why popular mass-market novels are written at a 7th grade reading level or lower. These top authors know exactly what the public wants.

LANGUAGE CHOICE CAN HELP YOU REACH THE MASSES

If you're still not convinced that you should *dumb down* your writing, then check out this quote from Elon Musk below. Musk is the CEO, founder, inventor, and adviser for some of the world's most successful technology companies, including Tesla, SpaceX, and SolarCity.

When Musk introduced the Tesla Powerwall in April of 2015, he knew that the general public was listening and not just engineers and other so-called *smart* people. Therefore, he tailored his presentation accordingly by using the following words:

> "This is how it is today," Musk showed a photo of a power plant spewing carbon into the air. "It's pretty bad. It sucks. This is real. This is actually how most power is generated, with fossil fuels."

Musk continued:

> "The solution is in two parts. Part one, the sun. We have this handy fusion reactor in the sky called the sun. You don't have to do anything. It just works. It shows up every day and produces ridiculous amounts of power."

Musk went on to say:

> "But here's the problem: the damn thing disappears at night. So if the world is going to go solar, it needs batteries. More specifically, it needs new batteries, because current batteries kind of suck. In fact, they're just really horrible, not to mention pricey and unreliable. And to top it all off, they're sort of stinky, ugly, bad in every way."

Eventually, Musk revealed the Tesla Powerwall which is a home battery backup system that captures sunlight from solar panels and converts it into energy. Although it's a highly complex device, its end user is the average consumer.

So Musk knew that he had to explain how the Powerwall worked and why people needed it by using very simple words.

If you examine Musk's language closely, you'll notice that there wasn't any technical jargon or difficult words to understand in his presentation. Every person who heard Musk speak could easily grasp the concept behind the Powerwall and how the technology worked without having to have a background in engineering. His language was so simple, even a fourth grader could understand it. I know this because I ran the text through a Flesch-Kincaid readability test.

FLESCH-KINCAID READABILITY TESTS HELP YOU WRITE BETTER CONTENT

The Flesch–Kincaid readability tests are a set of tests designed to indicate how difficult a passage in English is to understand. Musk's presentation scored a 4.3 on the Flesch-Kincaid Grade Level readability test (i.e. a fourth grade reading level).

If you want to know what the reading level of your affiliate content is, you can scan it through a free Flesch-Kincaid readability checker online. There are many free ones available. So just search for it online.

If your affiliate content scores higher than a 7th grade reading level, then you should consider stripping out technical jargon and other language that's difficult for the average person to understand. Doing this will allow more people to comprehend your content, which can lead to more affiliate product sales.

In my writing, I like to go one step further by simplifying it to a 3rd grade reading level if I can. That way, I ensure that everyone who lands on my affiliate pages can grasp the information I'm sharing regardless of their education level. The secret to doing this is by using short sentences and words with one syllable in addition to stripping out the technical jargon.

Here's an example of a paragraph that's on a 3rd grade reading level:

> "This space heater is cheap. I like it the best because of the digital thermostat. Not all cheap models give you this feature though. With it, you can pick the exact degree. Just choose any number between 65 to 85 degrees. It also turns off when the room reaches the right temperature."

Now compare that example with this one below which has a 9th grade reading level:

> "This is one of the least expensive space heater models available. What intrigues me most about this particular device is the digital LED thermostat control panel. You won't find this advanced feature on many other space heaters at this price point. The advantage to having a digital thermostat control panel are twofold: first, you can pick the exact degree for your heating comfort (i.e. 65 to 85 degrees), and second, it sends a signal to shut off the power to the unit when the room reaches a certain temperature level."

As you can see, this second paragraph is a lot more wordy and contains *smarter* sounding words. While it provides the same information to the reader, the first example is easier to comprehend and you walk away from it with the same amount of knowledge. Plus, it reaches a wider audience because more people can understand the language.

USING DESCRIPTIVE LANGUAGE HELPS COMPREHENSION

Keep in mind that it can sometimes be impossible to write affiliate content without technical jargon when you're listing out the features and benefits of the products you're reviewing. In those cases, you can do something like Musk did in his presentation by following up the complex words with a simple explanation that anyone can understand, as you'll see on the page.

Here's an example of how Musk did just that with the word "fusion reactor" which most people have no idea what it is:

> "We have this handy fusion reactor in the sky called the sun. You don't have to do anything. It just works. It shows up everyday and produces ridiculous amounts of power."

Now imagine if Musk had used this definition from Wikipedia instead:

> "Fusion power is a proposed form of power generation that would generate electricity by using heat from nuclear fusion reactions. In a fusion process, two lighter atomic nuclei combine to form a heavier nucleus, while releasing energy. Devices designed to harness this energy are known as fusion reactors."

That Wikipedia definition is much more complex and difficult for the average person to grasp. It also scores a 12.56 on the Flesch-Kincaid Grade Level readability test, which indicates a 12th grade reading level. As a strategic move, Musk took the complex term of a fusion reactor and made it easy to comprehend for anyone in the audience by relating it to something we all know about: the sun.

Let's now go back to my previous example of the space heater and apply what you just learned. Space heaters have a lot of technical words attached to their product descriptions because they're mechanical devices. Two words that pop up often to describe space heaters are "convection" and "wattage".

If I wanted to use those complex words in a product description on my affiliate page so that everyone who was reading it could understand them, then I could do something like this:

> "This space heater works by convection, which basically means it heats up the air. The maximum wattage is 1500W so it uses just as much electricity as any other space heater you can buy today."

After reading that paragraph, you easily know what the words "convection" and "wattage" mean without me having to give you the technical definitions. It's clear that convection means heating up the air and wattage means electricity use. You also know that most space heaters use up to 1500W of electricity. And even if the definition wasn't obvious, you can still gather that all space heaters use an equivalent amount of electricity without having to know what the word wattage means or even the specifics of 1500W.

The big idea here is that if you can reduce the language of your affiliate pages to a 7th grade reading level or lower and follow up any technical jargon with descriptive language that anyone can grasp, then you can make your content more understandable for the masses. And by doing so, you can improve your product click-through rates and conversion because your readers won't have to go to another site to clear up any confusion. Instead, they'll get everything they need to understand the complexities of any product on your well-thought-out affiliate page.

In the end, you're not actually *dumbing down* your content but making the language easier to digest. And when you do that, you're reaching more people which can lead to a boost in your affiliate product sales.

SECRET #8

USE ONE SENTENCE PARAGRAPHS (AT MOST TWO)

Back when I was in 6th or 7th grade, I learned how to write a proper paragraph in English class.

Perhaps you remember that same paragraph structure?

A basic paragraph consists of five sentences: the topic sentence, three supporting sentences, and a concluding sentence.

Does that ring a bell?

If not, just trust me.

We'll be throwing that advice out the window when it comes to writing your affiliate content.

You see, there's a better way of writing the paragraphs on your affiliate pages that can help people enjoy the content more.

And the more people enjoy reading your affiliate pages, the better chance you have at increasing your product click-through rates and conversions.

So that's what this chapter will teach you.

HOW TO WRITE BETTER PARAGRAPHS FOR AFFILIATE CONTENT

In journalism class, students are taught to keep sentences as short as possible, and one sentence paragraphs are considered perfectly acceptable.

Just pick up any newspaper or go to any major media outlet's website and you'll see one sentence paragraphs everywhere.

You might even see one or two word paragraphs.

Like this.

So why did I tell you that we were going to throw out proper paragraph structure when it comes to writing your affiliate content? Because we live in a mobile world now and most people are consuming content on their smartphones.

And reading paragraphs that are five or more sentences in length on a mobile device is rough. It looks like a wall of text that won't end when you're scrolling through the page.

In a physical book like this, it's fine to have long blocks of paragraphs because the user experience is different.

But not on websites.

When you're writing affiliate content, you should stick to one sentence paragraphs or two at the max.

Following that guidance will make your affiliate pages easier for people to read and digest.

And your readers will appreciate you much more for it.

A SIMPLE CSS TRICK

Finally, if you do start using this writing method and your content starts looking like a string of single sentences lined up on the page, then your website's font size is too small.

To fix that, you can adjust your site's CSS file to make the font attributes bigger.

For example, you can boost your website's font size to 18px or more. Then, change the line-height to 1.6em so there's enough padding between the top and bottom of the sentences.

A combination of CSS styles like that will boost your text size and make it easier to read for most of your visitors to read on a desktop computer and mobile device.

By the way, I only used one or two sentence paragraphs throughout this entire chapter so you could see how it looked in practice. Did you notice?

SECRET #9

VARY YOUR SENTENCE LENGTH

If you haven't had any professional training as a writer, then you've probably never thought about sentence length before. Most likely, you just write the words that come into your mind and put them down on the screen in the form of sentences.

While that style of writing does work, you can sometimes fall into the habit of writing a whole paragraph or more of sentences that are all the same length. And that can be a problem for your affiliate content.

Why?

Because if your sentences are all about the same length, then the text becomes boring to read. And as an affiliate marketer, you can't afford to have your content be boring.

If your content is dull, then more people will bounce from the page without making a purchase.

And that can kill your affiliate earnings.

So this secret is all about varying the length of your sentences and how you can use this tactic to create more engaging content.

WHY VARYING SENTENCE LENGTH IS IMPORTANT

I give full credit for this content writing secret to Gary Provost.

Gary Provost (November 14, 1944 – May, 1995) was an American writer and writing instructor who authored the book, "100 Ways to Improve Your Writing: Proven Professional Techniques for Writing with Style and Power (1985)", from which this secret was taken.

In that book, Gary explained why it's important to have variety in your sentence length and structure.

This famous quote from the book illustrates why:

> "This sentence has five words. Here are five more words. Five-word sentences are fine. But several together become monotonous. Listen to what is happening. The writing is getting boring. The sound of it drones. It's like a stuck record. The ear demands some variety.
>
> "Now listen.
>
> "I vary the sentence length, and I create music. Music. The writing sings.
>
> "It has a pleasant rhythm, a lilt, a harmony.
>
> "I use short sentences.
>
> "And I use sentences of medium length.
>
> "And sometimes when I am certain the reader is rested, I will engage him with a sentence of considerable length, a sentence that burns with energy and builds with all the impetus of a crescendo, the roll of the drums, the crash of the cymbals—sounds that say listen to this, it is important.
>
> "So write with a combination of short, medium, and long sentences. Create a sound that pleases the reader's ear. Don't just write words. Write music."

When I discovered this concept of varying sentence length and structure, I was blown away. I couldn't believe how something as simple as how long or short your sentences were could have such a big impact on the reader.

Once I learned this writing tip from Gary, I immediately went back through all of my top earning affiliate pages to vary the sentence lengths. After I did this, I noticed an improvement in the audience retention rate on those pages. By making my affiliate content more pleasant to read through the use of short, medium, and long sentences as well as giving it more rhythm, I was able to keep people engaged on my affiliate pages for longer periods of time. For example, the average time that users spent on one page went from 1:16 to 2:25 which was more than a 90% increase in reader retention. And that obviously lead to more affiliate product sales.

If you've never thought about varying your sentence lengths before, now's the time to do it. It's such an easy thing to implement and the results on your affiliate earnings can be dramatic. So give it a try!

SECRET #10

ASK RHETORICAL QUESTIONS

How would you like to boost your affiliate earnings by making one small tweak to your content?

If I told you that you could make more money just by asking questions to your readers, would you try it?

Well, that's exactly what this chapter is all about.

The affiliate content writing secret I'm going to share with you works like magic to persuade people to consider the comments you make on your affiliate pages more deeply. And the more you can get your visitors to actively engage with your content like this, the better chance you have at making affiliate sales.

The strategy I'm referring here to is asking rhetorical questions throughout your content. By asking rhetorical questions, you can subtly influence your audience's thoughts and opinions and persuade them to take the actions you want. So instead of just glossing over a particular aspect of a product review that could help you make a sale, you can make someone consider that information more carefully and click the affiliate link.

You can also use rhetorical questions in other ways throughout the page to increase reader engagement. We'll discuss those things and more in this chapter so you can work to improve the click-through rates and conversions on the affiliate products you promote.

WHAT IS A RHETORICAL QUESTION?

A rhetorical question is a question you ask for dramatic effect and don't expect an audible answer. At the beginning of this chapter, I asked two rhetorical questions. You can pick them out because they both ended in a question mark.

When it comes to asking rhetorical questions in your writing, there are several things that can occur: the answer may be obvious, there may not be an answer at all, or the answer is immediately given by the questioner (i.e. the writer). Regardless of the answer, the major benefit of using rhetorical questions in your affiliate content is that they can be used in a variety of strategic ways, including:

- Making the overall content more engaging for your readers.
- Influencing your audience to take a specific action.
- Emphasizing specific points in your content.
- Introducing new ideas.
- Forcing your readers to think deeper about certain topics.

By using rhetorical questions, you can essentially guide the thought process of your audience as they read your affiliate content. That's because rhetorical questions generate an implicit response in your readers where they feel compelled to fill in the gaps mentally. This persuasive form of writing can make your visitors consider what you say more carefully instead of just skimming over a particular part of your content.

WHY USE RHETORICAL QUESTIONS?

Good rhetorical questions will make your audience realize something that they weren't aware of initially. And that can entice people to keep reading the content on your affiliate pages and consider the things you have to say more deeply.

Rhetorical questions also have a compelling ability to make a person believe that they came to a conclusion all by themselves. Instead of you telling someone what to think, that person comes up with the idea on their own; even though you planted the persuasive seed in their mind. That's one of the most powerful ways to influence someone to agree with your thoughts or opinions and to take an action that you want, like make a purchase through your affiliate links.

As you may know, a lot of people don't like to be told what to do. They want to feel like they're in control of their lives, thoughts, and actions. So rather than just telling your reader what to buy outright, you can simply lead them to make that same conclusion on their own. By using rhetorical questions, you can subtly influence the kind of response you want from your visitors, be it good or bad. For example, you may want your audience to buy one particular product over another that's reviewed on the page because it's a better value or makes you a higher commission. Therefore, you can use rhetorical questions to conjure up a stronger desire for that product while making the other items seem less appealing.

In the end, when you use rhetorical questions in a strategic way, your affiliate content and product recommendations will feel more like a conversation and less like a lecture. And that persuasive power can help boost the engagement with your readers and your affiliate earnings.

HOW TO USE RHETORICAL QUESTIONS

There are three main ways in which you can use rhetorical questions in your affiliate content. And it's perfectly fine to use one or all of these methods on the same affiliate page. Just choose the tactic(s) that works best for each part of your content.

1. Emphasize a Statement

After you make a statement about something, you can use a rhetorical question to get the reader to think hard about that statement. This is a good way to emphasize a particular benefit or feature of a product so that the visitor has a stronger desire for it.

Here are a few examples of using rhetorical questions to emphasize a statement. I underlined the rhetorical questions so you can easily pick them out.

- This term life insurance plan offers $500,000 of protection. <u>Would that be more than enough money to take care of your grieving family for the rest of their lives?</u>

Examples Continued...

- The best part of this smart TV is the curved screen. With a curved screen, you'll feel more immersed in everything you watch because it replicates the sense of "real world" vision. <u>How would you like to have the best seat in the house no matter where you sit?</u>

- If you reserve a hotel room today, then you can get the luxury ocean view upgrade at no additional cost. <u>Is that $150 value worth passing up?</u>

2. Predict the Reader's Questions

As you're writing affiliate content, it's always good to predict the questions that your readers may have and answer them directly. By tackling questions ahead of time, you can work to eliminate doubt in people's minds. And if a person feels like they're getting all of the information they need to make a good decision, then your product conversion rates can go up. A rhetorical question is a great tool to help you with that.

Here are a few examples of using rhetorical questions to predict your reader's questions. I underlined the rhetorical questions so you can easily pick them out.

- As a cat owner, you may be thinking, <u>"What brand of food should I be feeding my cat to keep her healthy?"</u> The answer is Kitty Kibble, of course. It has the precise balance of nutrients to maintain lean muscle and vital organ health for your feline.

- Now you're probably wondering, <u>"How can I afford this $3,000 air conditioning system?"</u> Well, Acme Air Conditioners is giving first-time buyers a 12-month with 0% financing deal until the end of this month.

- <u>That all sounds great, but will this weight loss system actually work for you?</u> Yes! I haven't met one person who has NOT lost at least 10 pounds in the first month while trying it.

3. Enhance the Impact of Your Statements

Sometimes you may make a statement or claim about a product on an affiliate page and really want to enhance the impact of it. Rhetorical questions can help you with that as well.

By asking several rhetorical questions in a row after a statement or claim has been made, you can work to strip away doubt in your reader's mind.

Here are a few examples of using rhetorical questions to enhance the impact of a statement. I underlined the rhetorical questions so you can easily pick them out.

- This blemish cream has three acne-fighting ingredients while others only have one. <u>Wouldn't you like to have the clearest skin possible? Do you really want to waste time trying something less effective?</u>
- This 5-pack of dog bandanas includes these popular designs: dog bones, sun rays, autumn leaves, stripes, and snowflakes. <u>Don't they all look cute? Aren't they the perfect patterns for the entire year? Seriously, won't your pup look great in them?</u>
- My favorite feature on this dishwasher is the advanced cleaning sensor that lets you put even the dirtiest dishes inside without any worry about them getting clean. <u>Because who wants to waste time by pre-rinsing their dishes? Really? I don't. Do you?</u>

RHETORICAL QUESTIONS HAVE TO BE VALID TO WORK

One important aspect of using rhetorical questions that you need to be aware of is that they have to be valid for them to work. You can't use rhetorical questions to conjure up ideas that are unbelievable. Otherwise, this writing technique will backfire and make people question your authenticity and knowledge on a particular subject.

For example, suppose you're trying to convince someone to buy a new ping pong table. Ping pong tables are quite large and you need a lot of space to set one up. And while many ping pong tables can fold up nicely, you need a large spot inside a room to store them when they're not in use.

With that in mind, consider how strange these rhetorical questions sound below. I underlined the rhetorical questions so you can easily pick them out.

- With these adjustable dumbbells, you can change the weight between 5 to 25 pounds in a matter of seconds. <u>Don't you want to feel like an Olympian by lifting that much iron?</u>
- This ping pong table measures 6 feet long by 3 feet wide by 2 ½ feet in height. If you fold it up in half to store it out of the way, then it becomes 5 ½ feet in height by 1 foot deep. <u>Isn't that the perfect size to fit under your bed?</u>
- My favorite feature on this backpack blower is the 2.1 hp engine operating at 7500 rpms, which is capable of generating wind speeds up to 180 miles per hour. <u>Could you imagine blowing your neighbor's house down with it?</u>

RHETORICAL QUESTIONS ARE EXTREMELY VALUABLE IN AFFILIATE CONTENT

If you take the time to master the use of rhetorical questions, you can really drive the narrative in your affiliate content. Essentially, you can lead your readers to take notice of certain aspects of products, raise questions they might not have come up with themselves, and persuade people to take a particular action such as buying a specific item on the page.

The more you can emphasize your key points and get your audience to actively think as they read your affiliate content, the more engaged they'll be with it. And the more engaged a person is with something, the more value they place upon it. That's the hidden power behind rhetorical questions, and as an affiliate marketer, you can use them to your advantage to increase your product click-through rates and conversions.

If you want your affiliate content to resonate more with your readers, then sprinkle rhetorical questions throughout the page. One of the best places to start with this writing tactic is in the introduction. By adding at least one or two rhetorical questions in the introduction, you can immediately hook your readers. Predicting and asking questions upfront that you know your visitors are likely having can spark an immediate connection with them. As a result, people who land on your affiliate pages will instantly feel like they're in the right place because you already seem to *understand* them.

After the introduction, you can use additional rhetorical questions wherever you see fit. For example, if you're including some educational information before the product reviews, then you can place a few rhetorical questions within that section to highlight key points. Additionally, you can add rhetorical questions into the product reviews themselves. As I mentioned earlier in this chapter, rhetorical questions are a good way to get your readers to think more deeply about a particular product's benefits or features so they feel more compelled to buy it.

SECRET #11

USE EXPERT WORDS

What would you say if I told you that you could build instant credibility, trust, and influence with your audience—*in any niche*—without having to go out and get a professional certification or advanced degree?

Seriously, how would you like to boost your affiliate earnings just by sprinkling certain types of words throughout your content that make you *seem* like a top expert in your field?

If that sounds exciting, then you're going to love this affiliate content writing secret.

But before I get into the nitty gritty of how you can transform your content so it sounds like it's coming from an expert overnight, let me share with you why this tactic is so important in the first place. No matter what business you're in, be it affiliate marketing, blogging, direct sales, etc., before any prospect ever converts into a customer, that person must trust you. If they don't trust you, then you won't make a sale. Period.

Trust and credibility are so important when it comes to influence. If you're not trustworthy or credible, then people will question your motives and doubt your advice, which can cause you to lose a sale.

But winning a person's trust can be challenging, especially in a world where we're inundated with hundreds of marketing messages every day that proclaim "we're the best", "trust us most", "this is the #1 thing you've been looking for", etc. And that type of information overload makes it hard for affiliate marketers who are trying to prove to people who land on their pages for the first time that their product recommendations truly are the best that are out there.

So how do you position your affiliate site, company, or brand as the most trustworthy source in your niche? How do you make people instantly rely on your advice and recommendations for which products to buy? What can you do to stop your visitors from going elsewhere to confirm or deny the things you're telling them?

The answer to those questions is exactly what this chapter will teach you.

However, before I tell you exactly what to do, I want to share with you how I stumbled across this writing secret. Not only is it an interesting backstory for you to read, but it'll make you appreciate the tactic and trust the strategy behind it even more.

HOW I DISCOVERED THE SECRET OF USING EXPERT WORDS

About two years ago, an affiliate site of mine was ranking #1 in Google for some high volume and competitive keywords. One page in particular was making a boatload of money in affiliate sales as a result of those top rankings. But one day, Google decided to do a core algorithm update. And guess what happened? I lost all of those #1 ranking spots.

That incident came as such a shock too. I had been in position #1 for those target keywords for more than one year prior to that algorithm update. And in my mind, I was clearly the best affiliate content that was out there and did all of the right things to get to those top spots. However, Google suddenly seemed to disagree with all of that and my page dropped to positions #6-8 for every one of those target keywords.

As an affiliate marketer, I was so devastated by that incident. It was like someone had stolen my puppy! I lost about 60% of the traffic to one of my highest earning pages. And thousands of dollars in passive income that was being generated by those #1 ranking keywords vanished without warning. It was very sad and depressing. But being self-employed as an affiliate marketer, I couldn't just take that beating laying down. I depended on that income for survival. So for months, I tried different tactics to try to regain those #1 keyword positions. I did everything too, like build more backlinks, adjust my internal linking anchor texts, add more content to the pages, strengthen the on-page SEO factors, and more.

But nothing worked.

The pages kept sliding down the ranks and my top-earning page landed on the second page of Google for its most profitable keywords. I remember feeling the panic as that previous #1 ranking page dropped to positions #10-14 and then settled at around #16-20 for its highest traffic terms. I was completely confused too. I couldn't understand why any of the improvements I was making to that page weren't working to boost the keyword positions. So I scoured the Internet for solutions and even asked for help in SEO forums and Facebook groups, but no one had the answer. Everything people told me to try, I had already performed and none of it worked.

Then about two months later, I had a lightning strike of inspiration.

"What if the reason I wasn't ranking high anymore was because Google didn't think that my affiliate page was trustworthy?", I wondered. "Perhaps that latest algorithm update included more dependency on trust signals."

Up until that day, I thought that I had done a good job of making my affiliate site seem trustworthy and credible. I had all of the external factors in place like citations, social profiles, backlinks from high profile sites in my niche, etc. I also had internal factors for credibility such as a strong about page, author bio, privacy policy, contact information, and links to authoritative resources on each affiliate page.

After having that inspirational moment, I realized that some other crucial element must be missing. So I immediately searched for the target keywords for my top-earning page and made a list of the top five sites that were now ranking for those terms. Next, I studied every word on those pages. If a word or concept appeared on two or more of those sites, then I wrote it down.

I spent days doing this type of analysis—inspecting the content of my competitors in extreme depth.

Eventually, I discovered something that I had never noticed before. The pages that now ranked for the high traffic keywords I used to dominate had one thing in common that my page lacked. Something so simple too, and it was right in front of my eyes the whole time. I just didn't know to look for it.

What I uncovered was that the new top ranking sites were using *expert* words in the content. And these expert words seemed to be giving my competitors a huge ranking advantage.

WHAT ARE EXPERT WORDS?

As you might have guessed from the name, expert words are specific words that make you seem like an expert on a particular topic. And my page that used to rank #1 for certain high traffic keywords didn't have those expert words at all. In fact, when I look back to how my content was written for that page, I was lucky that I ranked so high for those keywords in the first place. That's because my page lacked words that demonstrated my expertise on the subject.

What are these expert words I'm talking about?

They include words like:

- Test(s)
- Research
- Lab(s)
- Results
- Data
- Claim(s)
- Measure
- Certified
- Certification

Expert Words Continued...

- Proven
- Trust
- Trustworthy
- Expert(s)
- Professional(s)

Every single site that jumped ahead of me in the search results after that Google core algorithm update had some combination of those expert words on the page.

A pattern that I exposed was that the dominant use of expert words was within the first 200 words of content (i.e. the introduction). And while some sites did have expert words scattered throughout the rest of the page, it didn't seem to matter for how high the page ranked for the target keyword.

That discovery was very surprising to me. I would have thought that the site which used expert words throughout the entire content would have been judged as a more authoritative resource by Google. But that wasn't the case. As long as some expert words were used early on in the content was all that seemed to matter to demonstrate credibility on a topic.

After analyzing multiple keywords, I felt like the writers for those high-ranking sites had discovered a hidden secret to stealing the top positions in Google because *all of their affiliate pages* used expert words in the similar manner. However, no one was talking about this tactic openly with other affiliate marketers online. The high-ranking sites I'm referring to here are ones like Forbes, Good Housekeeping, The Wire Cutter, Business Insider, and Consumer Reports. If you take a look at any of their top ranking affiliate review pages, then you'll see exactly what I'm talking about. Each one of those pages includes expert words like the ones I listed earlier in this chapter.

BACK TO THE STORY...

Once I realized this crucial piece of information about using expert words in affiliate review content, I immediately changed the introduction on my top-earning page that had dropped in rankings for its highest traffic keywords. What I did was included some of the same expert words that the top five competitors were using on their pages.

Then I resubmitted the page to Google Search Console, and waited.

And waited...

And waited...

I waited for several weeks and nothing happened.

I was so bummed.

I thought I had figured out the secret trick that only a select few individuals knew about for snagging the top spots in Google. But it seemed like I was completely wrong.

Then something amazing happened.

After about 30 days of waiting, my rankings finally improved. Out of nowhere, my top-earning page shot up from positions #16-20 to #6-12 for the highest traffic keywords. I couldn't believe it. That page finally popped back onto page one in Google for its most profitable keywords.

My theory on using expert words worked!

Now you may be thinking, "That's great, but you didn't make it back to the #1 position for any of your keywords." And while that's true, I actually reclaimed a lot of the lost income from that top-earning page even though it was only in positions #6-12 for most of the keywords. Technically, I didn't have to rank #1 anymore for any particular keyword in order to make a ton of money from that affiliate page.

Here's why that was the case...

Once I filled my money page with expert words, the content immediately became more trustworthy and credible with my visitors.

People now had more confidence that my site was a top authority in its niche. And this quality made it easier for me to persuade my audience that the products I recommended would be the best for their needs. By including those powerful expert words on the page, a lot more of my readers felt like they didn't have to go to other sites for additional information because I sounded like a top expert in my field.

This positive side effect of making more money from lower ranking pages was astounding. It just seemed to good to be true. So I had to confirm my findings by testing this theory on using expert words on other affiliate pages.

And sure enough, it worked.

Each page that I added expert words to performed better in product click-through rates and conversions than pages that didn't have those types of words. So I took this newfound knowledge and went through all of the affiliate pages on every one of my sites and updated the content to include expert words. The strategy I used was to place expert words throughout the entire affiliate page in ways that seemed appropriate without just trying to stuff them in there. I didn't just put expert words in the introduction like many of my competitors had done.

During my research, big name sites that were ranking in the top spots in Google, like Forbes, Good Housekeeping, The Wire Cutter, Business Insider, and Consumer Reports, didn't necessarily do that extra step, but I chose to incorporate it as a way to make the entirety of my content seem authoritative. My thought process was that Google may decide to adjust their algorithm one day to look for even stronger on-page signals of credibility and this strategy would hopefully work in my favor.

HOW TO USE EXPERT WORDS

I hope my story got you excited about trying this affiliate content writing secret. As you learned, it worked well for me and it can hopefully work for you too.

Now harnessing the power of expert words in your affiliate content is not that hard to do. In fact, all it takes is just a few expert words placed throughout the page to give your visitors the impression that your site is an authority on a particular topic.

Below you'll see the use of expert words in action. Use these examples to help you generate your own ideas for how to use experts words in your affiliate content. I underlined the expert words in each sentence so you can see where I placed them.

- That's why the <u>lab experts</u> at Fishn' Bros dug deep into the <u>research</u> to find the best electronic fishing lures on the market. Some fishing lures <u>claim</u> to be the best, but our <u>tests</u> indicate otherwise.

- Are you looking for a <u>proven</u> system that actually works? Not just some mediocre program that makes false promises? If so, this tried and <u>tested</u> system is what you need to get fast <u>results</u>.

- In this review, we're going to cover the top 10 infrared heaters you can buy today. After spending 22 hours doing intensive <u>research</u>, our <u>experts</u> determined that out of the 37 infrared heaters they examined, these were the 10 best products you can <u>trust</u> to keep you warm all winter long.

- If you want our <u>professional</u> opinion, this body massager is the only one you'll ever need. It has more than 2,000 positive reviews on Amazon and is <u>proven</u> to relax any part of your body. After <u>testing</u> it ourselves, we wholeheartedly agree that it meets all of the amazing <u>claims</u> that people are raving about.

- Before we recommend any product on our site, we search far and wide to find every <u>expert</u> opinion available on medical alert systems. And once we've performed the most in-depth <u>research</u> possible, then, and only then, do we add a product to our the top 10 medical alert systems list. As you'll find out below, we used five important criteria to <u>measure</u> the effectiveness of each device. You'll find the individual <u>results</u> next to each product review in the list.

- Why should you <u>trust</u> us? Because we don't just make false <u>claims</u> that can't be backed up like other sites do. All of the information we present here is based on the opinions of real-life <u>experts</u>, intensive <u>research</u>, and measurable <u>data</u>.

- Curious about what the <u>professionals</u> say regarding this accounting software? "It's the top choice for small business owners," explains Jeff Dawson, a <u>certified</u> CPA.

I hope you can see from those examples just how easy it is to incorporate expert words into your affiliate content. And once you try this affiliate writing secret, you won't believe the impact that expert words can have on your product click-through rates and conversions.

This is one of my best kept secrets in affiliate marketing and I've never shared it with anyone before writing this book. So enjoy the benefits of using this tactic on your own affiliate site and don't tell anyone else about it either!

SECRET #12

QUOTE SOMEONE

In the last chapter, I shared my personal story about how I discovered the hidden power of using expert words in affiliate content. This was something that the top ranking sites were doing that I wasn't. And by adding certain kinds of expert words to the page, I was able to elevate the sense of trust and authority for my content in the eyes of Google and my visitors.

During the course of that research, I also uncovered something else that the highest ranking sites were doing to further establish their credibility. And that was using quotes. If you check out the top ranking sites for many high traffic buying keywords, you'll see that most of the big name brands that have those spots are using quotes on the page. These are sites like Forbes, Good Housekeeping, The Wire Cutter, Business Insider, and Consumer Reports. Each one of their affiliate buying guides are quoting a person in some form or fashion within the content.

At first, I didn't pay much attention to the quotations I came across on those top ranking affiliate pages. They just seemed arbitrary. But as I analyzed my competitors more and more, I noticed a distinct pattern. Once again, it seemed like the writers for those big brand sites knew of a secret trick that was helping their affiliate pages rank higher in Google and generate more sales from their visitors by using quotes on the page.

So I incorporated that same strategy into my own affiliate content so I could maximize my earnings. And now you'll find out how you can do that too.

WHAT IS A QUOTE?

Quotes are using the speech or text from another person within your content while also acknowledging that person as the source for the information. I used quotes in this book in chapters #7 and #9 when I referred to the speech that Elon Musk gave in a presentation and the text that Gary Provost had written on how to improve your writing.

As you saw in those two examples, quoting someone can be done in two primary ways:

1. Quoting a person that gave a speech or was interviewed on a particular topic and crediting them as the source.
2. Copying a passage of someone else's written text or words and crediting them as the source.

WHY USE QUOTES?

In all types of writing, you can use quotes to provide evidence in support of your claims. And adding quotes on an affiliate page is a simple way to add that extra layer of credibility that can make your content as a whole seem more trustworthy.

By using quotations from other people to back up important concepts in your content or a product review, you can make those arguments more convincing for your readers. If other people—*especially experts*—agree with something you're writing about, then it's easier to persuade your audience that it must be true.

What's even more interesting about using quotations in your writing is that many people are influenced by quotes without even knowing who the cited person is. The quote doesn't have to be from someone famous or well-known in your industry. Just the act of quoting someone gives the appearance that your content is more trustworthy because a third-party is commenting on the topic at hand.

If you found the previous paragraph hard to believe, I assure you that it's true.

Just think about the last piece of journalism you read or listened to. That content probably had at least one person quoted in it to back up a claim or statement that was made in the piece. News reporters depend on the use of quotes in their content because they're not experts in a particular field. They also want to report objectively. So news reporters must rely on the testimony or written word of others to report the facts for a particular story and establish credibility with their audience.

It's the same reason why using quotes in your affiliate content can be so powerful. The general public is accustomed to seeing—*and believing*—quoted individuals, and you can tap into this asset to make your affiliate content more trustworthy and credible in the eyes of Google and your visitors.

HOW TO USE QUOTES IN AFFILIATE CONTENT

There are three main ways in which you can generate quotes for your affiliate content. And you can use one or all of the methods described below on each affiliate page you publish.

1. **Interview an expert in the field or someone else who has firsthand experience in the topic.** This is the most credible way to get a quote for your affiliate content. Just find a person who can make a statement that helps support the most important claims that you're making on the page.

   For example, if you were trying to sell a piece of medical equipment, then you could contact a physician and ask them some questions about the benefits of that product. And with their approval, you could then use those answers as quotes in your article while crediting the physician as the source.

   Here's an illustration for you to see how this idea works: "I would recommend this brand of knee scooter to my patients because it provides excellent relief for weight-bearing recovery periods," said Dr. Marvin Gupta, MD, orthopedic surgeon for the Battlefield Hospital in Kentucky. "You can also check with your insurance company to find out if it will cover the cost of the knee scooter. Each insurer is different, so it is worth the phone call to save some money."

2. **Find someone who has already made a claim about a particular product or concept you're referencing on your affiliate page.** This is the next best way for getting quotes. You can search the Internet for experts who have already been quoted about something you want to highlight in affiliate content. Just be sure to quote the original source for the quote and link back to it so that they can get some credit. It's not good practice to just steal quotes from other sources.

   For example, the U.S. Environmental Protection Agency is often quoted for this statement, "Americans, on average, spend approximately 90 percent of their time indoors, where the concentrations of some pollutants are often 2 to 5 times higher than typical outdoor concentrations." You can find this text directly on their website under the *Indoor Air Quality* section. News reporters use this quote a lot in their stories on air pollution, which seems to be a hot topic during certain times of the year.

3. **Add a quote from someone who represents your company or provide one yourself.** By far, this is the easiest method for getting a quote. And while it may seem to be self-serving, it still gets the job done. If you work for a company that's publishing the affiliate content, then just find someone inside that business who can offer an opinion on the subject at hand. Then quote that individual on the page and list their name and job title as the source. If you're the sole owner of your affiliate business, then you can still take advantage of this method for generating quotes by adding a citation from yourself. And don't be scared to try this method either. I see this strategy used all of the time on big brand websites that have affiliate pages. So it can definitely work for you too.

   For example, here's how Good Housekeeping quoted themselves on an affiliate buying guide for air purifiers, "The effectiveness of air purifiers in real-world situations likely won't mimic those of controlled conditions in a lab," says Rachel Rothman, chief technologist at the Good Housekeeping Institute.

And here's how Consumer Reports did the same thing on a competing affiliate page on air purifiers, "The best air purifiers we tested clean the air quickly and perform well on the quieter low speeds too," says David Trezza, CR's lead tester for air purifiers.

Perhaps you're the lead tester for your own affiliate products? If so, don't hesitate to add in your own opinions as quotes to your content like the other big brands are doing. They do it because it works. And you can take advantage of this same strategy too.

HOW MANY QUOTES SHOULD YOU USE?

Now that you know why quotes are important and how to use them in your affiliate content, the next logical question you may have is, "How many quotes should I use on each affiliate page?"

The answer is that you can use as many quotes as you want.

However, during my research and testing, I discovered that using at least two quotes is a good minimum for each affiliate article. If you look at the affiliate pages of the top brands I mentioned earlier, you'll see that they all use at least two quotes in their content. Often, it's the same person giving those quotes too. But not always. Sometimes it's a combination of one external source and one internal source for those quotations. Therefore, you can do whatever you think is best for your affiliate pages as for who to quote.

For example, you could find a quote online from an expert who has already been cited on a topic that relates to your affiliate content and include it on the page. You could also insert your own opinion on the same matter to back up that expert's claim or refer to something else on the page like in a product review.

Your options here are limitless. There are so many different ways in which you can combine internal and external sources for quotes for maximum impact on your affiliate content. Just be creative and use the methods for generating quotes that work for you.

USE QUOTES EARLY ON

Another important tip I'd like to share is that you want to try and add at least one quote within the first 300 words on your affiliate pages. And, if you have an external source for a quote, then you should give preference to using that one first.

Starting your content out with a quote will immediately boost the credibility of it. You don't want to wait until you get to the product reviews section—*or later*—to add in your quotations. If you do that, then the quotes you use will have less of an impact on your readers. The goal is to start out your affiliate content strong and let people see that your page is trustworthy with resources that can back up the claims you're presenting. You want to give your visitors the impression that your affiliate content is well researched and comprehensive on the topic, and quoting people early on is the best way to do that.

QUOTES CAN IMPROVE READER ENGAGEMENT

I hope you enjoyed this content writing secret and are now thinking of ways to incorporate the use of quotes on all of your affiliate pages. For me, this strategy has not only increased my product click-through rates and conversions, but it has also boosted the average time people spend on my affiliate pages. By quoting other people and myself, my visitors take the content more seriously, and therefore, are more engaged with it. Readers also feel more comfortable with the product recommendations I make because I've displayed that I've done thorough research on the subjects I'm writing about by including supporting comments by other experts. And if other experts are agreeing with me on a particular topic, then why wouldn't my audience accept the things I have to say as true?

It's a win-win situation when you use quotes in your affiliate content. So give it a try!

SECRET #13

LABEL YOUR READERS WITH A NOUN

I came up with the idea for this affiliate content writing secret after reading the book, "Monster Loyalty: How Lady Gaga Turns Followers into Fanatics" by Jackie Huba.

For those of you who don't know who Lady Gaga is, she's a pop musician with a cult following. And in that book, Huba explains how one of the most influential ways that Gaga was able to cultivate her fanatical group of fans was by giving them the name, "Little Monsters". This name is what allowed her hardcore followers to self-identify with everyone else who was part of the Lady Gaga superfan group. And that one simple attribute is what helped her fan base explode beyond measure.

After learning about that powerful concept, I looked into the marketing strategies of other popular musicians to see if anyone else was using that same tactic of labeling their fans to build a stronger presence. What I discovered was that many of the top artists of our time were, in fact, using that same fan-labeling trick.

I then looked into other areas of pop culture to see if this same strategy of identifying people with a particular label (or noun) applied to things like movies, films, TV shows, books, sports teams, etc. And to my surprise it did. There were "fandoms" popping up everywhere I looked.

So I used this same tactic to improve the engagement rate and earnings on all of my affiliate sites, which I'll show you how to also do here.

WHAT IS A FANDOM?

A fandom is a subculture that's composed of fans who are characterized by a friendship with others who share a common interest. Fandoms can grow out of any interest or activity too. Fandoms can be narrowly focused on a single thing, like a musician (e.g. Lady Gaga), or encompass an entire genre or hobby (e.g. travelers). Basically, fandoms consist of people who are fascinated with a subject or activity and self-identify with the other people who are equally as passionate with it.

Here are some examples of popular fandoms that you may recognize:

- The Beatles: Beatlemaniacs (musician)
- Bob Dylan: Dylanologists (musician)
- Cleveland Browns: Dawg Pound (sport)
- Doctor Who: Whovians (TV show)
- Game of Thrones: Thronies (TV show)
- Glee: Gleeks (TV show)
- Green Bay Packers: Cheeseheads (sport)
- Grateful Dead: Deadheads (musician)
- Harry Potter: Potterheads (movie)
- KISS: Kiss Army (musician)
- Lord of the Rings: Ringers (movie)
- Star Trek: Trekkies (TV show)
- People who like to travel: Hodophiles (hobby)
- People who love food at the highest level: Epicures (hobby)

FANDOMS ARE LINGUISTIC LABELS IN DISGUISE

The more I dug into this idea of fandoms, the more I found out that many of these fanatical group names were manufactured by the marketing departments of these various musicians, movies, TV shows, sports teams, etc. And while these fan names may seem like a fun thing to identify with, the truth is that these names are being used to tap into a persuasive type of psychology called "linguistic labels".

Below is an excerpt from the research article I found on the topic of linguistic labels, "Being What You Say: The Effect of Essentialist Linguistic Labels on Preferences" by Gregory M. Walton and Mahzarin R. Banaji. This excerpt will help you understand why linguistic labels can be so powerful in marketing.

> "Three experiments examined the effects of essentialist linguistic labels on perceptions of preferences of others and of the self. In Experiment 1, participants evaluated the preferences of others described with noun labels (e.g., "Susan is a chocolate-eater") as stronger, more stable, and more resilient than those described with descriptive action verbs ("Susan eats chocolate a lot"). Experiments 2 and 3 revealed the analogous effect for self-perception: participants evaluated their own preferences that they had described with nouns (rather than verbs) as stronger, more stable, and more resilient. These results indicate that the very manner in which attitudes are expressed can affect their status and evaluation. Linguistic forms that imply essentialist properties (e.g., nouns) can engender the inference that such attitudes are dispositional and therefore strong and stable. More generally, these results show that attitudes are plastic constructions shaped by subtle but pervasive cognitive and social input from the environment."

The key takeaway from that research on linguistic labels is that you can create a stronger affinity with your audience if you label them with a catchy noun. By labeling your readers with a word that they self-identify with, you can make your content connect with them better. As people read your affiliate page, they'll feel more in tune with your message and that can lead to higher product click-through rates and conversions.

HOW DO LINGUISTIC LABELS APPLY IN AFFILIATE MARKETING?

Now you don't have to go overboard and create some super fancy fandom name like the examples you saw earlier in this chapter for musicians, TV shows, movies, and sports teams. The idea of using linguistic labels effectively in affiliate content is much more subtle, which I'll explain here.

I'll give you a few examples below so you can see what labeling your readers with a noun looks like in practice. That will help the idea behind this psychological concept of using linguistic labels make more sense.

Consider these statements:

- Jessica likes to play video games.
- Ben loves distance running.
- Kelly has a lot of cats.
- Ted tries to be productive.
- Jason goes to the gym every day.

Each of the statements above emphasize the verbs. Those statements tell you what the person *does*.

Now consider these statements:

- Jessica is a gamer girl.
- Ben is an ultra runner.
- Kelly is a fur momma.
- Ted is a productivity fiend.
- Jason is a gym junkie.

Each of these statements emphasize the nouns. The statements tell you who the person *is*.

While both sets of statements convey the same meaning, the second set has a much stronger impact because they create an identity for the person by using a noun (i.e. label). By labeling each person with a catchy noun, your audience will conjure up a picture of what that person is like based on common stereotypes.

The other benefit of labeling your readers with a noun is that it can instantly make your content seem more relatable to your audience. For example, if you have an affiliate buying guide on the best gaming controllers for girls, then the person who's reading your content is most likely going to be a female. And that person probably considers herself a "gamer girl" even if she doesn't go around saying it to others. Internally, she relates to the idea of being a gamer girl.

Now imagine if that same girl was to come across your affiliate buying guide on the best gaming controllers for girls and saw this introduction:

> "What are the best gaming controllers for girls? In this post, I'll share the top 10 products that are good for female gamers. By the end, you'll have a good idea on which one is right for you."

That introduction is not bad, but it's not great either. Compare that text with this version below:

> "Are you a gamer girl? Do you want to compete with the other gamer boys and beat them to oblivion? If so, you can up your chances of total domination by using one of these top 10 best gaming controllers for girls. As you'll see below, the sizes of these controllers are made specifically for girl-size hands so you can hit your button combinations faster and with more accuracy. By the end, you'll have the perfect idea on which controller is right for your gamer girl playing style."

As you can see, this second version does a much better job of hooking the reader into the content because it uses the idea of linguistic labels. If a girl who loves to play video games was to read that introduction, she would instantly connect with the content because it uses the label "gamer girl" to identify with her. And the better you can connect your content with your audience, the more they'll keep reading your affiliate page and feel comfortable taking your advice and product recommendations.

MORE EXAMPLES OF LINGUISTIC LABELS

We'll now look at a few more examples of incorporating linguistic labels in affiliate content so you can see how labeling your readers with a noun works in various niches. The samples you'll see next will also serve to help you generate your own ideas for using linguistic labels in your affiliate content. I underlined the nouns so you can easily pick them out.

Original: Are you a person who's in need of some new photography gear?
Modified: Are you a photog who's in need of some new photography gear?

Examples Continued...

Original: For people who want the most amount of bass out of their speakers, this model has the lowest frequency range.
Modified: If you're a true <u>bass head</u>, then you'll want this model since it has the lowest frequency range.

Original: Alright home cooks! Making pounds of your own fresh pasta just got a whole lot simpler with this Cuisinart device.
Modified: Alright <u>foodies</u>! Making pounds of your own fresh pasta just got a whole lot simpler with this Cuisinart device.

Original: If you want to be a better pool player, then you'll need a cue stick tip that's made with eight layers of 100% Japanese pig leather.
Modified: If you want to be a real <u>pool shark</u>, then you'll need a cue stick tip that's made with eight layers of 100% Japanese pig leather.

Original: As a professional landscape painter, you know how important it is to select paints with the highest quality pigments.
Modified: As a professional <u>landscapist</u>, you know how important it is to select paints with the highest quality pigments.

After reading those examples, you should now understand how subtle —*and powerful*—the use of linguistic labels can be for your affiliate content. As you saw in those samples, all it took was a slight change in how we referred to the target audience who's reading the page to make a stronger connection with them.

In the original versions, the sentences were a bit too generic. They didn't grab on to the reader in any meaningful way. On the other hand, the modified versions labeled the readers with a noun that they could easily identify with. And once a person associates with that noun, all of the words that follow it are instantly more compelling because they feel like they've been written specifically for that individual.

Labeling your readers with a noun is a simple way to transform lackluster content into something that's more personal and relatable to your visitors, which can help to improve your product click-through rates and conversions.

FINAL ADVICE ON USING LINGUISTIC LABELS

Before I end this chapter, I wanted to share two more pieces of advice on how to best use this idea of linguistic labels in your affiliate content. By following this guidance below, your content will have a better chance of coming across as natural and appealing for your readers.

1. **Try to label your readers with a catchy noun as early as possible on the page.** The earlier you can hook your readers with this noun, the more they'll relate to your content and want to keep reading it. Therefore, it's best to work that noun into the introduction for maximum effectiveness. It wouldn't do you any good to wait until the middle or end of the post to start labeling your readers with that noun.

2. **Don't overuse the noun you choose to label your readers with in your writing.** There's no exact science behind how often you should use the noun, but when it's used too much it'll come across as a gimmick. A handful of times scattered throughout the page is all you really need to make your readers feel more connected with your content.

By using linguistic labels strategically throughout your affiliate content, you can make your pages much more relatable to your readers. And the more engaged a person is with your affiliate page, the more they'll trust what you have to say. In turn, they'll feel comfortable clicking on your affiliate links and purchasing the items you recommend.

SECRET #14

BAIT YOUR READERS WITH A HOOK

In 2008, the Nielsen Norman Group published the article, "How Little Do Users Read?", and one of the main takeaways from that content was that the average person only has enough time to read *at most* 28% of the words during a website visit, but with 20% being more likely.

While I couldn't find a more recent study that quantified how much or how little people spend reading text online, I can only assume that it might even be a lower percentage today. That's because we live in a mobile world where we consume most of our content on our smartphones and many different things are competing for our attention.

On the web, we don't read in the same manner as we read books or magazines. We don't pour over every word and read text in a strictly linear fashion. Instead, we scan the words on web pages looking for things that perk our interest or can give us a quick gist of what the full piece of content is about. In short, most of us are very impatient readers online.

However, one part of a web page that many people do tend to read is the introduction. The reason being is that this section of the page gives people a glimpse of what the rest of the content is about. An introduction is your first impression for your visitors. And you only get to make it once.

If the information in your introduction appeals to the person reading it, then they'll stick around to read more of the page. If not, they'll leave.

So it's very important that you craft your introductions so they immediately hook your reader's attention. Otherwise, you might not get your visitors to read the rest of your content. And as an affiliate marketer, it's essential that you get as many people as possible to read your pages so you can turn those readers into buyers.

But how do you write an irresistible introduction that makes people want to read your content all the way through?

That's what we'll cover here.

HOW TO HOOK YOUR READERS WITH THE INTRODUCTION

There are three ways you can craft your introductions on your affiliate pages so they suck people into your content. I'll cover each method separately along with examples on how to use them well.

1. Open with a Question

Opening with a question is the simplest way to start any affiliate page. What's good about asking questions is that it forces your readers to mentally respond to them, which creates an instant dialogue with your visitors. By asking questions, you can hook your audience into your content and compel people to want to read more.

There are two ways to use this method of asking questions.

The first method is to ask questions that you know people are seeking answers to by coming to your page. That way, the visitors will instantly feel like you understand them because it's like you're *reading their mind*.

The second method is to ask questions that spark curiosity but not provide the answers. This style forces your visitors to keep reading the page as a way try and resolve that tension. People can't stand when they don't know the answers to things and you can use that internal conflict to your advantage to get more people to continue reading your content.

Examples of Using Questions in Introductions

Below are a few examples of how questions can be used effectively in an introduction to hook people into reading more of the content.

- How would you like to lose 20 pounds in the next month? Would you be excited if you could do it without giving up carbs? Well now you can with this revolutionary new weight loss program.
- Is your dog hard to train? Are you looking for a training method that will actually work on your stubborn pooch? If so, this dog training guide can help to finally relieve that unnecessary stress.
- Do you want to double your email open rates? How about boosting the click-through rates on the links that are inside of those emails? If that sounds exactly like what you're looking for, then you'll love this new email software reviewed below.
- What if I told you that I could help you find a cheap baby stroller under $100 that rivals the more expensive versions? Would you give it a try? Or at least see what it has to offer?
- Can you really pay half price for an airline ticket? Or is that just a myth that these online brokers use to lure you into a higher-price ticket sale? The truth may surprise you, which we'll reveal here.

2. Start with an Interesting Fact

Facts are another way to hook people into your content. But the facts you use must be interesting or shocking for them to work. If you include boring facts in your introductions, then people won't be as excited to read the rest of the page.

The other important thing to keep in mind here is that the facts you use need to relate to the page's content or niche. For example, you wouldn't want to use a fact about monkeys on an affiliate page that talks about rice cookers. That would just be odd.

To find good facts to use in your introductions, you can do a Google search for your topic's niche + "interesting facts" or "surprising facts". This should return a list of results for you to sift through to find something unique to use on your affiliate pages.

Examples of Using Interesting Facts in Introductions

Below are a few examples of how interesting facts can be used in an introduction for a food-related affiliate page.

- Did you know that scientists can turn peanut butter into diamonds? It's true! Peanut butter is so rich in carbon that it's actually possible to turn a jar of Skippy into a flashy diamond necklace. According to scientists at the Bayerisches Geoinstitut in Germany, all you need to do is to extract the oxygen from the carbon dioxide found in the peanut spread, and then enact immense pressure on the carbon that has been left behind. And voila! A shiny new diamond for you to enjoy!
- Fun fact: Fruit snacks and cars are coated in the same type of wax. Sounds icky doesn't it? Well, how do you think your favorite gummy bears get that glossy sheen? They're coated with carnauba wax which is the same type of wax used on cars to protect the paint.
- How do maraschino cherries, strawberry desserts, and even red Skittles get their red coloring? From the crushed carcasses of a beetle known as the Dactylopius coccus, of course. Carmine, also known as carminic acid, is a common red food dye that's made from those beetles. Sounds yummy, doesn't it?
- 40% of food is wasted in the United States every year. That's almost half of your dinner plate dumped straight into the trashcan.
- It takes 660 gallons of water to make one hamburger, according to the U.S. Environmental Protection Agency. You can see why swapping your beef hamburger for a veggie burger is not only a healthier choice but also one that can save a ton of water too.

3. Use an Anecdote

Another way to start your affiliate page introductions is with an anecdote. Anecdotes are short stories about a person or real incident that are amusing or interesting. The main purpose of using anecdotes is to draw your readers into your content by making them laugh or think more deeply about the topic at hand.

Anecdotes are a sure-fire way to get people's attention because they make your affiliate content more relatable.

But what makes a good anecdote?

One method is to mention your own experience with a product you're reviewing or something that happened in your own life that relates to the subject matter of the content. Not only does this help establish you as the expert on a particular topic, but you also get to decide how to apply the story and what it means to your readers.

Another method is to start with a funny incident or a touching moment. If you can make people laugh or cry at the start of your introduction, then your audience will have an immediate emotional connection with you and want to keep reading.

No matter how you craft your anecdote, keep in mind that it has to set the scene so the reader can visualize where something is happening—like a problem or action. People love to read stories and using anecdotes is a simple way to hook your visitors into reading more of the content on your affiliate pages.

Examples of Using Anecdotes in Introductions

Below are a few examples of how anecdotes can be used in an introduction to hook people into the page's content.

- I once had a German shepherd. He was extremely smart too. Each morning, I'd open up the front door and he'd run out, pick up the newspaper, bring it back into the house, and set it down on the sofa. The sofa is where my wife would enjoy her first cup of coffee in the morning while reading the newspaper. That German shepherd made sure that she had the newspaper by 6:30 a.m. every single day. But my dog wasn't always that smart. I had to try several different dog training programs until I found one that worked. I'll share my experiences with you here about each program and reveal the top dog training course that finally beat them all—and made my wife *the happiest woman on earth.*

Examples Continued...

- I can still remember the sound of the screaming crowd as we made the final touchdown with 5 seconds left on the clock. It was 1997, and the odds were 50:1 that we would ever win a single football game that year. But we were the ones who ended up taking the trophy. We went from being in last place to becoming the local champions for our football league. Now you might think I'm crazy when I say this, but I believe that a big part of that radical transformation was due to the new football equipment we received that year. Here's what I mean...

- Two years ago, I was searching for a set of adjustable dumbbells. Although I had a gym membership at the time, I still wanted the convenience of working out at home. So I spent several weeks looking at all of the different brands of adjustable dumbbells you could buy online. Most were priced between $300 to $500, but after a lot of digging, I discovered a fantastic set of top rated adjustable dumbbells for around $150 with free shipping. What brand were they? I'll show you below. But first, let's talk about the features you need to look for in a high-quality set of adjustable dumbbells so you know exactly why the ones I chose were a great deal.

BONUS TIP: WRITE YOUR INTRODUCTION LAST

While the introduction is the first impression a reader gets when landing on your affiliate page, it should be the last thing you tackle as the writer. What I mean by this is that you should attempt to write your introductions only *after* you've written the bulk of your affiliate content. Once everything is written, you'll have all of the key information fresh in your mind. And that cluster of ideas can help you craft a better introduction than if you tried to write the introduction first.

If you start the writing process with your introduction, you may realize later that your content has taken an unexpected turn, the tone has changed, or your understanding of the topic is different than before you began. That's why you should make it a habit to write your introductions last. Only after the entirety of the affiliate content has been written will you know the best way to approach your page's introduction.

As you learned at the beginning of this chapter, website visitors only read about 20-28% of a web page. And as an affiliate marketer, your main goal is to get your readers to stick around and hopefully read more than 20% of your pages so you can make a sale. A well-crafted introduction that immediately hooks the reader in is the best way to do that. Therefore, you should put a solid amount of thought and effort into the introductions of every affiliate page you publish. By doing so, you can increase your product click-through rates and conversions.

Finally, don't be afraid to change your introduction from time to time if you're not getting good results for a particular affiliate page. If the bounce rate on your page is high or the average time visitors spend on the page is low, change up the introduction to see if it helps improve those metrics. For example, if you used the method of asking questions in the introduction, then try new questions. Or, if you started with a fact, try a new fact. Or, if you began the introduction with an anecdote, then try removing it and using questions or a fact instead.

You'd be surprised at how a small tweak or two in your introductions can get people to stay on your affiliate pages longer. And it's often one of the simplest ways you can squeeze more profit out of the visitors who consume your affiliate content.

SECRET #15

PUSH YOUR VISITORS TO READ MORE

As humans, we have a strong desire for closure. For example, we don't like it when stories in books are interrupted or unfinished. We also can't stand it when we try to get a hold of someone and they're not available. Similarly, if we miss a phone call from a friend and they don't leave us a message then that causes us to worry about what they may have wanted. And finally, it drives many of us nuts having to wait for the next episode of a TV show when we're left with a major cliffhanger at the end.

The need for getting closure is ingrained in all of us. We can't stand ambiguity. It creates a strong curiosity in our minds. And if we don't get that closure, our minds continue to race about the issue at hand. It's hard for us to stop thinking about things if we haven't received clear answers to them.

It's that very reason why we binge watch certain TV shows and can't bear to put down some books while we're reading them. The producers of those shows and the writers of those books know just how much the lack of closure drives us to watch show after show and reach chapter after chapter. But what we're not privy to here is that the producers and writers behind these popular TV shows and books have mastered a concept called the "open loop". And open loops are a powerful way to entrance people with a piece of content.

In this chapter, you'll find out how to use this same idea of open loops to your advantage on your own affiliate pages.

WHAT IS AN OPEN LOOP?

An open loop is a common tool that writers use when telling stories in the written and visual form. Our brains naturally want to seek out some sort of conclusion when we're presented with ambiguous details and the open loop is what creates that anticipation and also provides the eventual conclusion we desire.

You can use this same tactic of open loops that produce a strong desire for closure in your affiliate content to push your visitors to read more. By using open loops, you can keep your readers more engaged and scrolling through the page. And the more time a person spends on your content, the more likely they are to buy something.

But how do you exploit the human desire for closure in your affiliate content by using open loops?

We'll cover that next.

HOW TO USE OPEN LOOPS

There are two steps in the process of using open loops in your writing:

Step 1: Make a statement that sparks curiosity

The first statement must be something unique, shocking, or over-the-top. The purpose here is to create curiosity in your reader. You want them to feel compelled to find out the answer behind whatever you stated.

Step 2: Reference an upcoming point of closure

After curiosity is sparked, a second statement is made that will motivate the person to continue reading your content so they can resolve the ambiguity. This is where you'll bait the reader by referencing an upcoming point of closure without actually stating when they'll get it. This is what creates the anticipation and desire to seek closure.

By following this two-step process, you can essentially keep your visitors on the edge of their seats as they read your affiliate content.

EXAMPLES OF USING OPEN LOOPS

Below are some examples of the two-step open loop process in action.

- Last year, I tripled my affiliate income by making one small SEO change. More on that later.
- In 2018, the most advanced rifle scope was invented, and it had two particular features. I'll explain what those are below.
- With a clever cooking tool, I could patty out a full plate of hamburgers for the entire family in 30 seconds. You'll see how it works in a few paragraphs.
- Before you buy a new wireless thermostat, you need to make sure that your existing thermostat connection has a certain set of wires. If your house doesn't already have these wires run, then you can't use a wireless model. You'll find out what that wiring setup is in this guide.
- I went from having $3 in my bank account to more than $100,000 in just 30 days. How did I do it so fast? I'll share the exact method in just a minute. But first, let me tell you a story...

As you can see, the first sentence or two of each example states a unique, shocking, or over-the-top claim. Those statements create a desire for you to want to learn more. But then, the last sentence of each example references the upcoming point of closure without telling you exactly when you'll get it. Therefore, you must keep reading to find out the answers.

That's a pretty cool trick, isn't it?

Now one of the best places to start using open loops in your affiliate content is in the introduction or directly after it. By making a statement that sparks curiosity in your reader's mind, but not explaining the answer behind it, you can push your visitors to want to read more of the page.

What's also nice about this writing technique is that you can use it over and over again throughout the entire page as a way to keep your readers engaged with your content. An easy way to do that is by creating an open loop in your introduction and closing that loop a bit farther down the page by revealing the answer. Then, right after you close that first open loop, you make another statement that sparks curiosity to create another open loop. That will compel the reader to keep scrolling to find out that answer. And when they do, you'll close that loop and have an opportunity to open another loop again if you choose to do so.

EXAMPLES OF REPEATEDLY OPENING AND CLOSING LOOPS

Below are some examples of opening and closing loops throughout an affiliate page that sells robot vacuum cleaners. These samples are meant to be excerpts from a full buying guide.

- There's one robot vacuum in particular that can do much more than just clean the dirt off your floors. In fact, it can replace most of your floor cleaning tools because it includes one extra advanced feature that not many other robot vacuums have. What is that feature? I'll show you in my #1 review below.

(In the #1 product review, the reader finds out that it's a wet mop feature. The open loop that was previously created would then be closed. Another open loop can then be created by using the next statement in that same #1 section of the review.)

- As you can see, this model can both vacuum up dirt and wet mop your floors. So you get the best of both worlds. But it's about $100 more expensive than our #3 review that has a slightly similar feature.

(The visitor has been hooked to find out what the similar feature is in the #3 product review. The person must keep reading to find out the answer. In the #3 review, it's revealed that you can upgrade a cheaper robot vacuum model to include the wet mop feature. It doesn't come with that function by default. The open loop would be closed after learning this bit of information. Another open loop can then be created in this #3 review section by using the next statement.)

- While this cheaper model can be upgraded to include the wet mop feature, you'll have to pay about $50 for the extra part. If you're not interested in wet mopping, then you should also consider our #5 review. It's almost identical in functionality to this model, but the #5 version includes an additional benefit that's usually only found on the more expensive robot vacuums.

(This new open loop will make the reader want to find out what that additional benefit is, so they'll keep reading until they get to the #5 product review. In the #5 review, it's discovered that this model includes a Wi-Fi app for wireless control. The open loop would then be closed. Another open loop can be created in this #5 review section by using the next statement.)

- If you're looking for the best overall value in a robot vacuum cleaner, then this is a great model to choose because it has a Wi-Fi app. However, you can get a lot more cleaning power out of it if you follow our list of robot vacuum cleaner tips in the next part of our buying guide. So be sure to take a quick look at that section.

(The reader will most likely want to know how to get more cleaning power out of this #5 robot vacuum model. So they'll go and check out the tips section of the page. The open loop would then be closed after the person reads the tips.)

As you saw in those examples, you can create open loops throughout your entire affiliate content to drive someone to read the whole page. Instead of just hoping that a person comes to your page and reads all of the product reviews and information in the buying guide section, you can use open loops to hook their interest and drive that curiosity to learn more.

ANOTHER WAY TO USE OPEN LOOPS

You can also use open loops in a block format at the beginning of your affiliate content to spark—*and extend*—the reader's curiosity. This is done by adding an enticing set of bullet points into your introduction. Then you reveal the answer to each open loop statement one by one throughout the course of the page.

The next page includes an example of how to use this method of opening several loops in one block at the beginning of an affiliate page.

This illustration below uses the same type of information that was given in the last set of examples for opening and closing loops throughout an entire page. It has just been adjusted to be in the block format with bullet points.

> In this robot vacuum cleaner buying guide, I'll show you what the best robot vacuums are for your home. After 15 hours of intensive research and testing, I've narrowed it down to the top five models that will meet most everyone's needs. In particular, you'll discover:
>
> - A robot vacuum that can replace all of your other floor cleaning tools, including the mop.
> - A model that's much cheaper than any other product you'll find today, but gives you the added advantage of upgrading it at any time to have the same set of cleaning features as the most expensive robot vacuums.
> - A low-priced robot vacuum that includes an advanced feature that's usually only found on the high-priced models. Hint: It's like a remote control but on steroids.
> - Plus, a list of the top 10 tips you can use to get extra cleaning power out of any robot vacuum you choose—even the cheap ones.

As you can see, there are various ways you can use this writing strategy of creating open loops effectively in your affiliate content. And it's one of the best kept secrets for pushing visitors to read more of the page.

Like you've learned elsewhere in this book, the more time you can get your visitors to stay on a page, the more engaged they'll be with your content. And that can lead to an increase in click-through rates and conversions for the products you promote.

SECRET #16

PICK 3 PRODUCTS TO BE YOUR ALL-STARS

This is one of my top secrets for making the most money on each affiliate page I publish and I'm excited to share it with you. It's a concept I came up with after noticing a strong pattern on which products sell the most on my affiliate sites.

If you're creating a traditional affiliate buying guide that lists the best products in a specific niche, then you're most likely promoting between five to ten items on that page. Top five to top ten lists seem to be the sweet spot for ranking high in Google for target keywords and meeting the needs of interested searchers. However, you have to be very strategic about the products you do promote on these types of guides and the order they're listed on the page if you want to maximize your affiliate earnings.

I often see affiliate buying guides that are ranking on the first page of Google for a competitive keyword that promotes each product on the page equally. It's as if the person who wrote the article had no clear opinion on which product is truly the best out of all of the items they're reviewing. And that approach can be bad for your bottom line as an affiliate marketer. If you don't encourage people to choose one particular product over another that's reviewed on your affiliate page, then that person might not know which item is right for them. And if that happens, the visitor will probably leave your site without making a purchase.

I've talked to a lot of other affiliate marketers who have top ranking pages for many high traffic keywords, but their conversion rates are lower than expected. After a quick audit, I could clearly see that they don't make it easy for their visitors to make a quick buying decision. So even though these affiliate pages get a ton of traffic, they're not earning nearly as much money as they could because of how the product lists are structured.

A simple solution to this type of problem is to choose three products to be your all-star items and then focus on promoting them the most.

CHOOSING YOUR 3 ALL-STARS

No matter if you're promoting five products, ten products, or even more on a single affiliate buying guide, you need to follow this one crucial piece of advice: *pick three items that are going to be your all-stars*.

What I mean by this is that you want to choose three products that are going to be your top choices for people to purchase that affiliate page. Then you want to use the right language and content structure to entice people to buy those three things.

Now if someone does buy one of the other products listed that are not your all-star items, then that's fine too. You still make money. However, you're going to focus the majority of your efforts on persuading people to pick one of your three all-star products because that will help you write more persuasive content that can lead to higher sales.

A good strategy for picking your three all-stars is to choose one item in each of these categories:

1. The most expensive item with the most features.
2. The least expensive item with the best features.
3. An item with a moderate price and a moderate set of features that offers a good overall value.

By choosing three all-star products according to that previous criteria, you've essentially met the general consumer demand for online shopping. Some people like to buy the best-of-the-best product no matter how much it costs; that would be item #1. Others want the cheapest option they can find that also has a good set of features; that would be item #2. And finally, some people want a middle-of-the-road choice that doesn't cost too much and has a good range of functionality; that would be item #3.

CHOOSING THE OTHER ITEMS TO FEATURE ON THE PAGE

If we lived in a perfect world that wasn't controlled by search engine algorithms, then writing an affiliate page with those three all-star products you chose would likely give you the highest earnings from your content. That's because you would be offering options for every type of buyer, and therefore, meeting the general consumer demand.

But in my experience, you need to have at least five to ten products on an affiliate buying guide just to compete for high traffic buying keywords. Having a page with only three product reviews won't work well to capture those top keyword spots.

In the past, things were different. I actually used to structure all of my affiliate pages with only three items because I earned more money that way. However, my rankings started to slip after a few Google algorithm updates and the competing pages that ranked higher than mine included more individual product reviews. So I had to add more items to my pages just to compete against the other sites that were ranking. But I still follow the same rule of choosing three all-star products to focus on as a way to maximize my affiliate earnings on each page I publish.

If you're writing a top five to top ten list buying guide, then you have to select some more items to complete that list. However, the other items you choose to include on the page don't matter all that much once you have those three all-star products picked out. Your main goal is to get people to buy one of the top three all-star items.

Now continue on to the next chapter where I show you how to write the descriptions for those items to generate the most affiliate sales.

SECRET #17

APPLY THE FEATURE STACKING TRICK

In the last chapter, I recommended that you select three products to be your all-stars when you're putting together a top five to top ten style buying guide. I also mentioned how it's not a good practice to make every single item on the page equally as valuable in your visitor's eyes. If you do that, then the person may get confused on which product is actually best for their needs and not make any purchase at all.

The common term for this phenomenon is "choice overload" which is a cognitive process in which people have a difficult time making a decision when they're faced with too many options.

As an affiliate marketer, your goal is to reduce confusion for your visitors so that you can encourage people to take action now by purchasing something through the links on your site. When you do that, you can experience higher click-through rates and conversions on the products you promote.

This chapter will teach you how to do just that.

HOW TO ORDER YOUR ALL-STAR PRODUCTS

If you want to make the most money from the all-star products you chose, then you need to order these items on the page in a certain way. By doing so, you can encourage people to purchase more of them.

First, structure your page so that you review those three items in this order:

1. The most expensive item with the most features.
2. The least expensive item with the best features.
3. An item with a moderate price and a moderate set of features that offers a good overall value.

By sticking with this order, you're following the logical path in a typical consumer's mind. Most people want to know what the best-of-the-best product is up front. And some of those people will buy that item no matter what else is being featured. Plus, this top item will give the reader a baseline to compare all of the other products that are reviewed on the page.

Many of your visitors who don't want to buy the most expensive item will quickly look for the cheapest product that can offer just as good of an experience. That's why you review the least expensive item as the second product on your list.

Finally, after people find out what the best (and most expensive) item is and compare it to the cheapest item they see, they often want to know what another good alternative is for their money. That's why you list the middle-of-the-road item third on your list. This product meets the desire of people who want to feel like they're getting an overall good value for their money. They may not want to buy the best or most expensive thing out there, nor do they want to get the cheapest version available. That's why the third pick is beneficial in this place on the list because it meets the needs of this type of consumer.

WHAT ABOUT THE OTHER ITEMS?

If you're creating a top five to top ten style buying guide, then the order of the other products being reviewed outside of your three all-stars doesn't matter too much. Just put those items in any order you think is best. As I've stated before, these other products don't really matter in the grand scheme of things. Most people tend to buy the same few products no matter how many you review. That's why this secret on choosing three all-star products to focus on can help to improve your bottom line as an affiliate marketer.

APPLY THE FEATURE STACKING TRICK

Now that you know how to order the products you're reviewing on the page, the next step you should take is to apply the feature stacking trick. This trick taps into the natural buying habits of consumers.

Consumer psychologists have discovered that people perceive a long list of features on an item as being more valuable. So you can make a product appear to be a better choice just by adding more features to it. Therefore, you should list out as many features as possible for your #1 top all-star pick. Seriously, go all out here. Come up with as many things as possible that you can point out for the best and most expensive product on the page.

The list of features you choose can be written out as bullet points or in paragraph form. The style doesn't really matter, so it's up to you on how you want to list them out. But in either case, the description for your #1 top pick should be the longest and most feature packed content on the page.

When you write the description for your #2 top all-star pick, which is the least expensive item with the best features, make this product stand out as well with a long list of features. However, scale the list back a bit by not giving it as many highlights as the #1 top pick. You want this #2 all-star item to be slightly less attractive than the best and most expensive product you review.

As for the description for the #3 top all-star pick, which is the moderately priced item with a good set of features, keep this list of features about the same as the #2 top pick. You want this product to be just as appealing as the cheaper item but not more enticing than the #1 top pick.

By following this feature stacking trick for your top three all-star products, you're essentially making these items appear to be the most attractive for your readers. When your audience reads the descriptions of these all-stars, they're getting an overwhelming sense that each one can deliver a great value for their money. And by the time your visitors get done reading the top three product reviews, each person should have a good idea on which item is best suited for their needs and budget.

Unfortunately, any other product listed on the page outside of those top three all-stars becomes a distraction to making a sale. As you learned in the beginning of this chapter, the more options a person has when making a buying decision, the more that person experiences choice overload. And if choice overload is too severe, then the person won't likely buy anything in that moment. What they'll do instead is leave the page to do additional research or spend time offline thinking about what choice they should actually make.

MAKE THE OTHER ITEMS LESS ATTRACTIVE

In order to reduce consumer choice overload and improve your affiliate sales, you'll want to make the descriptions for the other products you review on the page not as detailed as the top three all-star items. Essentially, you want all of the other products to be less attractive to your visitors.

If you used long sets of bullet point lists in your top three all-star picks, then make the bullets much shorter for the other competing product reviews. For example, if you have ten strong features listed for your #1 top pick, then you might want to include only three key points for the #4 and #5 product reviews. Additionally, make each description shorter and shorter as you review each subsequent item. So items #6 to #10 on a top 10 list would have the least number of features highlighted.

By following this type of strategy, you're subconsciously telling the reader that the products you're reviewing are becoming less and less important as the list goes on. And the more you can make those additional items seem less appealing, the more your visitors will be encouraged to buy one of the top three all-star products on the page.

FEATURING STACKING CAN BE VERY PERSUASIVE

You'd be surprised at just how powerful this feature stacking trick can be to convince someone to buy a product of your choice. As the writer, you get to choose what things to include for each product you review on the page. And by feature stacking, you're letting the reader know that the top products you recommend are the best options for them to consider. So it becomes a no-brainer for which ones to choose between.

The truth is that you can't recommend five to ten things equally. If you did that, then your reviews wouldn't be very trustworthy. When it comes to reviewing products in any niche, there are clear winners and losers. That's just the facts.

By using the feature stacking trick, you're actually doing your visitors a favor by sorting your top five to top ten buying guide lists for them. And the easier it is for your visitors to make a good decision, the more comfortable they'll feel making a purchase through your affiliate page.

So make it a habit to apply the feature stacking trick on every affiliate buying guide you publish. By doing so, you can experience higher product conversion rates and an increase in affiliate commissions as a result of it.

SECRET #18

FOCUS ON THE PERSON, NOT THE PRODUCT

When it comes to affiliate marketing and product reviews, there are two approaches you can take. The first is to focus on what a product is or does (i.e. the features). The second is to focus on how a product will improve a person's life (i.e. the benefits).

But which of these two approaches do you think is more effective at making a sale?

If you chose how a product will improve a person's life, then you were correct. Selling the benefits of a product is much easier than trying to convince someone that an intangible feature is worth a higher price. Therefore, when you're writing your affiliate content, it's better to focus on the outcomes that a product can produce for a person rather than the product itself. By helping people visualize how a particular item is going to improve their lives, you can increase your click-through rates and conversions on every product you promote.

So what's the real difference between features and benefits and how do you apply this strategy in your own affiliate content writing?

We'll cover all of that and more in this chapter.

WHAT IS A FEATURE?

Simply put, a feature is something that a product has or is.

Features are the technical specifications that make up a product. A list of features tells you what you'll get when you buy a particular item. When you see a list of features, it's up to you to decide which ones are the most important for you.

A good example of a feature is a *rechargeable battery* on a power drill. Other examples of product features include a *5TB hard drive* on a laptop, an *18-inch blade* on a chainsaw, and a *rear windshield wiper* on an automobile.

WHAT IS A BENEFIT?

A benefit is the result that a person experiences when using a product feature. The benefits are the actual reasons why a customer buys a product.

A good example of a benefit is the *length of time* a person can use a power drill with a rechargeable battery. When a person buys a cordless power drill, they're purchasing it for convenience. They don't want the hassle of being tied to an extension cord like you get with a standard electric drill. If the power drill can give the user the freedom to drill things for up to two hours at a time without being near a power outlet, then that can be a great benefit for the operator.

Other examples of product benefits include *the peace of mind* a father gets when buying a $500,000 life insurance policy that will take care of his family's needs when he dies, *the countless hours saved* with a grocery store that offers free home delivery, and a blend of yogurt that *improves your digestive system* by including high-fiber nutrients.

Although it might seem counter-intuitive, people rarely buy things for the included set of features. Instead, they want products that solve their problems by offering attractive benefits.

COMBINING BENEFITS WITH FEATURES

Now you know what the difference is between features and benefits and why focusing on the benefits in your affiliate marketing is much more effective than highlighting a product's features. But how does this concept translate to your affiliate content to help you make more sales?

When you're writing your product reviews, you'll want to add a benefit statement for every feature you highlight. That way, the reader can get a better sense of how a product's features will improve their life.

To show you how this method works, let's take this list below of intangible features of a smart refrigerator and turn them into an exciting list of benefits for the reader:

- 28 cu. ft. of capacity
- Three internal cameras
- Touchscreen panel
- Three adjustable shelves
- Door alarm

Here's that same list of features with benefit statements added to them:

- With 28 cu. ft. of capacity, this refrigerator can hold enough food for 5 to 7 adults.
- The three internal cameras allows you to see and check the contents from anywhere inside the fridge without opening the door.
- The touchscreen panel lets you manage every aspect of your food, including the set up of expiration notifications, getting nutritional information, and planning meals with the items that are currently inside of the refrigerator.
- With three adjustable shelves, you can make room for even the largest dish. These shelves are incredibly useful during the holiday season too, like Thanksgiving, when you need to pack a lot of food containers of various sizes into a tight space.
- The door alarm will ensure that your food never spoils. If the door is accidentally left open for longer than 30 seconds, an alarm will sound so you know that cold air is escaping and you need to shut it.

As you can see, each feature has been attached to a benefit that can help the reader visualize exactly how they'll use the various functions of the smart refrigerator. If a benefit was not mentioned for each feature, then the person would have to come up with their own ideas on how they might use a particular function. However, if that person is not fully clear on what a feature does, then they may not even know how beneficial it can actually be for them.

For example, reading a technical specification about the refrigerator including a touch screen panel doesn't tell the person much about how it can be used to set up food expiration notices, get nutritional information, or plan meals with the food that's on hand. Without adding in that beneficial information, the reader may not even think that those things are possible with a refrigerator in today's modern world.

FOCUS ON YOUR READERS NEEDS AND ENJOY MORE SALES

Now that you're armed with the knowledge on how to jazz up your affiliate product descriptions with features that are packed with benefits, you should make it a habit to focus on the reader and not the product when you're writing that content.

You should also try to turn even the most boring product features into amazing benefits that the reader can latch onto. For example, the height and weight of a dehumidifier are not that exciting to read about; however, if you include that the dehumidifier only weighs 10 pounds, which means you can lift it effortlessly with one hand to transfer it from your bathroom to your bedroom, then that makes the weight seem impressive. It also gives the reader a better idea of how they might use the dehumidifier in their house. Plus, if you said that the dehumidifier is only 16 inches tall and that it can easily slide under any standard size desk or side table, then the person can also visualize how the unit can be used in various parts of the home without it getting in the way.

If you didn't include beneficial information like that, then the person may not have ever thought about the convenience that a dehumidifier of this size could offer them.

As you learned here, highlighting the benefits in your affiliate product reviews is one of the best ways to get people to want to buy those things you're promoting. And the more you can make an item seem beneficial in the reader's mind, the easier it is to get them to click on the product link and for you to make a sale.

SECRET #19

ALWAYS START WITH THE STRONGEST BENEFITS

In addition to highlighting the benefits of the products you're reviewing, as you learned in the last chapter, you also don't want to overlook the sequencing of those benefits. If you do, you could be leaving a lot of money on the table.

When you're writing your affiliate product descriptions, you always need to make sure that you lead with the strongest benefits for each item. This is especially true when you're reviewing your top three all-star products.

By putting the strongest benefits at the beginning of your product descriptions—or at the top of the bullet point lists—you can make the items you promote seem more enticing to your readers. And that can translate into higher click-through rates and conversions on the products you promote.

This short chapter will explain why that's true because of two psychological effects called "primacy" and "priming".

PRIMACY AND PRIMING EFFECTS

There are two psychology concepts that relate to this idea of putting the strongest benefits at the top of your product review descriptions. The first is called the "primacy effect" which is the tendency for people to remember the first piece of information they encounter better than the material presented later in a sequence. The second is called the "priming effect" which is when the first things we come across set the standard for everything else that follows.

Now without getting too technical with the science behind these two psychological effects, basically all you need to know here is that by using the ideas of primacy and priming, you can create a favorable first impression for a product that leads to a ripple effect for everything else you mention about that product throughout the review.

When your first benefit is strong, you raise the expectations for the remaining information. And those expectations generate a more favorable perception even if the additional benefits are not that exciting. Plus, people tend to remember the first things you mention about a product the most, so you can plant a seed for the benefits you do want that person to remember as they're reading the rest of your reviews.

I know that this secret may sound simple, but it works.

SECRET #20

KEEP YOUR NEGATIVES BRIEF

Up until this chapter, I've only mentioned the importance of using positive language to help sell more affiliate products. And while that guidance does work to increase your sales, it can also backfire if all you do is highlight the good things about every product you promote.

When people are reading product reviews, they want to know both the good and bad aspects of things. As with everything in life, nothing is perfect, and you can build a lot of credibility with your audience if you point out some of the negative traits that each product you recommend has.

However, there's a secret art to using negativity in a positive way so that you can still make a lot of sales.

That secret is what I'm going to share with you here.

HOW TO USE NEGATIVES IN A POSITIVE WAY

It's interesting to see so many high ranking affiliate pages in Google that include a pros and cons list below each product reviewed on the page. And while it may seem like a good idea to the writer to use such lists because it's being totally transparent with the reader, these pros and cons lists can actually reduce your conversion rates. By mentioning too many negatives about a product, you can turn a person off from wanting to buy it even if it's one of the best items available.

Additionally, if you mention an equal number of positives and negatives about every product you review, then you're making it much harder for your visitors to make a quick buying decision.

As you learned in chapter #17, people who are faced with choice overload will have a more difficult time making a purchase. That's why those long lists of pros and cons for every product on an affiliate page can make things very confusing for your audience. Your visitors will have to spend a lot more time comparing and contrasting multiple products to figure out which one actually meets their needs.

So if it's your goal to increase your product click-through rates and conversions, then it's better to be brief and mention only one or two negative aspects about each item you review. Doing this will give your readers the impression that you're being fully honest with them about the good and bad traits of each product. Also, your content will come across as more authentic and trustworthy, instead of appearing like you're just trying to make a sale by highlighting the positive attributes of every product you recommend.

The way I like to include negative aspects in my product reviews is to first list all of the positive benefits in each item's description. Then, I'll add in one or two sentences that point out some of the negatives. Finally, the last sentence of each product review will be something good so that I can end each description on a positive note.

On the next page, you'll find an example of that content writing strategy in practice. I kept the total review as short as possible to save space in this book. I also underlined the negative attributes and put the positive follow up statements in bold so you can easily pick them out.

EXAMPLE OF INCLUDING A NEGATIVE CHARACTERISTIC AND FOLLOWING IT UP WITH A POSITIVE STATEMENT

This Acme portable air conditioner is the best choice for apartment renters. Not only does it meet all of the various apartment building restriction codes, but it also doesn't have to be vented out a window. So your landlord won't even know you have it!

As for the top features of this AC unit, you'll get:

- 4 fan speeds to select the perfect amount of blowing air for your comfort.
- An ice compartment that lets you chill the air even more. Just dump in some ice and enjoy an icy cold breeze effect.
- Caster wheels for easy transport. You can literally roll this air conditioner from room to room with you, which allows you to buy just one unit to use everywhere in your apartment.

Now you may think that this portable AC unit is a dream come true. <u>But, it does have one tiny flaw. The noise level for the medium and high fan speed settings can be quite loud. So you'll want to operate it on the lowest fan speed whenever you can. Especially, if it's going in a bedroom.</u>

But for the price, you won't find anything better than this powerful air conditioning unit for an apartment. It tops the charts in every other way!

That was just one example of how you can include a negative trait for a product but still keep it brief. For anyone reading that description, they can see how beneficial this portable AC unit can be for their apartment regardless of the noise issue. And if anyone is concerned about the louder fan speeds, there's an easy workaround for it.

MORE EXAMPLES OF USING NEGATIVES WITH POSITIVE FOLLOW UPS

Below are a few more examples of how a negative aspect of a product can be immediately turned into something positive to help generate a sale. Again, I underlined the negative attributes and put the positive follow up statements in bold so you can easily pick them out.

- The battery on this cordless chainsaw only last about 20 minutes, which isn't a lot of time. **However, if you're not squeezing the throttle constantly, you can easily use it for one hour or more with stop-and-go cutting.**
- One thing this guitar amp lacks when compared to the other products on this page is a distortion knob. To get any type of distortion, you'll need to connect a separate pedal. **But the truth is that most skilled guitarists don't use the distortion feature on amplifiers anyways. You can't tweak the sound as much as you can with a dedicated pedal, so don't let that missing feature deter you from buying this model if you like it.**
- This tower fan lacks two features: a remote control and a timer. **But in all my years of owning a fan, I've never once used those things. So you're probably not going to miss them either. Plus, you can save $50 by buying this model over the last one I reviewed.**

From those examples above, you can see how adding in one or two negative qualities for each of those products can boost the credibility of the review. You also saw how easy it was to transform those negative traits into positives by using a strategic follow up statement. The basic takeaway for this chapter is that the more authentic your content appears, the more people will trust your product recommendations. And the more trust you can earn with your readers, the more affiliate commissions you can earn.

SECRET #21

IF YOU GIVE A STRONG WHY, MORE PEOPLE WILL BUY

In the last few chapters of this book, you learned how to craft better affiliate product descriptions so they make the items you recommend more attractive to your readers. While following that advice will definitely work to increase your sales, there's one extra step you can take to boost your conversion rates even more for the things you're trying to sell.

The concept behind this secret is something that took me a long time to discover, but after I did, my affiliate commissions skyrocketed. And after many months of testing the idea I'm about to share, I confirmed that it can work for practically every niche.

What I'm referring to here is giving your readers a specific reason for why they should buy one particular product over another. When people are trying to make a purchasing decision, they tend to grasp onto the things that help them shorten the buying cycle. So it's a good idea to make each product you're promoting stand out from the rest on each of your affiliate pages.

As you'll learn in this chapter, there are a number of key reasons why people buy things. And if you give a strong why, more people will buy.

10 MOTIVATING FACTORS FOR WHY PEOPLE BUY THINGS

There are basically ten reasons why people buy any product. Those reasons include:

1. To save time
2. To save money
3. To make money
4. To avoid effort
5. To escape pain
6. To gain comfort
7. To get praise
8. To feel loved
9. To improve health
10. To increase social status

If you can align your affiliate products with one or more of these reasons for why people buy things, then you can make it much easier for a person to make a purchasing decision. If a person feels like they can gain or avoid an internal want or desire by getting one of the items you recommend, then it will lower the resistance they have against making an immediate purchase.

As you're writing your affiliate product descriptions, think about each of those ten reasons why people buy things and ask yourself how they apply to the product at hand. To do this, just phrase those aspects as a question, such as "How does it save time?", "How does it save money?", "How does it make someone money?", "How does it give someone comfort?", and so on.

With some products, only a few of the top ten reasons for why people buy things will make sense. For other products, all ten may apply. Just go through the list of reasons for every product you're reviewing and make notes of your answer for each reason. If one doesn't apply, then skip it.

EXAMPLES OF HOW TO APPLY THIS STRATEGY

We'll now go over a few examples of this strategy so you can see how it works. That way, you can start applying it to your own affiliate content.

Example #1: Dog Training Video Course

Save time: With this dog training video course, you can train your dog much faster than using the traditional in-person method. You can get your dog trained in about five days versus spending 6-8 weeks with in-person training sessions.

Save money: This online program costs a fraction of the price that a real dog trainer charges.

Make money: After taking this course, you can sell your own services as local dog trainer.

Avoid effort: This video dog training course is much easier to digest and implement than reading a book. Plus, the course is taught by a certified dog trainer. So you're getting expert tips that work without having to sift through numerous books to find the best information.

Escape pain: This video training course can reduce your anxiety when you take your dog out in public because he or she will always obey you.

Gain comfort: Once your dog is trained using this system, your dog will obey your every command and you'll get much more enjoyment out of the time you spend with your pooch.

Get praise: After finishing this course, your family and friends will see you as an authoritative person who can maintain control over animals. You'll also be praised by other pet owners who can't get their dogs to obey them.

Feel loved: Dog owners who take this video training course feel much more connected to their pets. People who finish the course feel more loved and respected by their dog.

Improve health: Doesn't apply.

Increase social status: Doesn't apply.

Example #2: Rice Cooker

Save time: Buying this rice cooker means that you don't have to spend 20 minutes watching over a boiling pot on the stove. You can simply add water and rice to the machine and let it do all of the cooking for you. You can work on preparing other parts of a meal or go do other leisurely things while the rice cooker cooks perfect rice every time.

Save money: With this rice cooker, you can make rice more often because it's easier to do. In turn, this will save you money because rice is a cheap grain that can be added to any meal.

Make money: Doesn't apply.

Avoid effort: No experience is needed to use this rice cooker. You can make batches of rice without putting in much effort at all. If you can pour water into a container and add a scoop of rice, then you can have restaurant-style rice whenever you want it.

Escape pain: By using a rice cooker, you can avoid the hassle of over-cooking or under-cooking your rice. You can have rice with perfect texture every time.

Gain comfort: Doesn't apply.

Get praise: Doesn't apply.

Feel loved: Doesn't apply.

Improve health: Whole grains like rice can improve blood cholesterol levels and reduce the risk of heart disease, stroke, type 2 diabetes, and obesity. Brown rice also contains several additional heart healthy components, such as minerals, antioxidants, and dietary fiber. By using this rice cooker, you can add more rice to your diet, which can help to improve your overall health.

Increase social status: Doesn't apply.

Example #3: Electric Chainsaw Sharpener

Save time: With this electric chainsaw sharpener, you can sharpen your entire chain in a few minutes. Compare that with a manual sharpening file that can take one hour or more.

Save money: By sharpening your own chain with this tool, you can lower your costs of owning a chainsaw. New chains are priced anywhere between $20 to $50 each. By using this electric chainsaw sharpener, you can get more life out of your existing chain and save a substantial amount of money over the life of your chainsaw.

Make money: Doesn't apply.

Avoid effort: Owning an electric chainsaw sharpener makes sharpening your chain a breeze. With a manual file, you have to perform multiple strokes on each chain tooth to get it sharp. You also have to be very precise as you sharpen with the file. Mistakes can easily happen and your chain teeth might not be uniform or cut well afterwards. With this electric chainsaw sharpener, there's no effort involved. You simply attach the chain to the vise, turn on the grinding wheel, lower the wheel to the chain tooth, and let it sharpen for 2 seconds. Then, move on to the next tooth. It doesn't get much easier than that to sharpen a chainsaw chain perfectly each time.

Escape pain: Doesn't apply.

Gain comfort: Doesn't apply.

Get praise: Doesn't apply.

Feel loved: Doesn't apply.

Improve health: Doesn't apply.

Increase social status: Doesn't apply.

THE NEXT STEP OF USING THIS STRATEGY

After you're done asking yourself those ten questions about each product you're promoting, pick the top two or three reasons you think would be good to include in each item description. If the same reasons apply to more than one product you're reviewing, then just choose different answers for each item. Don't include the same reasons for every single product. Otherwise, there won't be much variety in your descriptions and each item will seem like they meet the same basic needs for every person.

Also, try to get creative. Perhaps, you can find an interesting angle or something else that's unique about a product that makes it stand out from the others on the page. Maybe one particular feature or benefit can be expanded upon and turned into a stronger reason for why someone should buy that item over another.

And finally, don't forget about the advice given in chapters #16 to #19. You still want to choose three items to be your all-star products and focus your best efforts on promoting those items. So make sure that those three all-star products have the best and most reasons for why someone should buy them. Then scale back on the other products you're reviewing by including only one reason or none at all. Otherwise, you'll make it harder for your readers to make a quick buying decision.

On my affiliate pages, I often leave out the top buying reasons for the last two or three products I review because they're not the items I really want my visitors to buy. Plus, this technique makes the other products on the page look better and reduces choice overload for my visitors so that I can make more sales. So give it a try!

SECRET #22

KEEP REFERRING BACK TO YOUR ALL-STARS

Another secret trick you can use to encourage people to buy more of your all-star products, is to refer back to them in each subsequent product description. The best way to do this is by picking out one or two features of the other items and comparing them to your all-star picks.

When you make comparisons like that, the reader can't help but think that the all-star products are an even better deal than they may have seemed before. That's because you're constantly referring back to those items and you're solidifying the reader's choice that one of those top three all-star products is truly the best choice for their needs.

It's a subtle marketing tactic, but it works.

Of course, some people will still buy one of the other items that are not your all-star products, and that's not a bad thing. You still earn an affiliate commission from those purchases.

But if you use the strategy outlined in this chapter for increasing the perceived value of those top three all-star products, then you can reduce the hesitation that some people might have when making a buying decision online. As I've stated before in this book, the more you can get a visitor to narrow down their buying options, the faster you can get them to purchase something, which means more money in your pocket.

EXAMPLES OF REFERRING BACK TO THE ALL-STAR PRODUCTS

Below are several examples of this affiliate content writing secret in practice. Just look for the reference back to an earlier product in each sample description.

- These wireless headphones are a good deal, but one thing they lack is an LCD screen with control buttons on the side like our #1 pick includes. That feature is nice to have because you can adjust the settings and see what you're doing without having to take the phone out of your pocket.
- If you're looking for a battery operated hedge trimmer that's easy to use, this is your best option. It's lightweight, has a comfortable handle, and an automatic shut off system if the trimming blades get clogged. However, the battery life isn't as long as our #2 recommendation which lasts up to 2 hours on a single charge. This product only lets you cut for 45 minutes.
- This 2-in-1 convertible laptop gives you the luxury of transforming your computer from a tablet into a fully functional laptop with a keyboard. It also comes with a 256 GB flash drive to store all of your files and media. It's quite similar to our #3 laptop review, but this one has a slower 1.8 GHZ processor. If speed is important to you, then you'll probably be happier with the 2.6 GHZ processor that comes with our #3 top pick.
- What you'll like most about this baby bottle warmer is that it accommodates every size bottle that's out there. This compatibility problem is a known issue for many brands of bottle warmers, so you don't have to worry about this product not working with your existing bottles. The only drawback though is that you can't choose a precise temperature degree like you can with our #1 top pick. This model only has an on/off switch for warming the water. If you care about getting a precise temperature for your baby's milk so it's never too hot, then you'll want to consider our #1 recommendation.

Did you see how adding a simple comparison and reference back to the top #1-3 picks in each of those descriptions made those all-star products seem like better choices? This is a simple trick that can be added to any affiliate page to help to increase those affiliate earnings.

YOUR EXISTING SALES DATA CAN HELP

If you've been in the affiliate marketing business for a while now, then you probably have enough data in your sales records to confirm that your visitors are only buying a handful of items that you recommend on each page. Certain products just drive more sales than others even without using the tactics I've outlined in this book. That's why I recommend that you focus your efforts on promoting three all-star products. Doing so will help you make more money in the long run.

With that sales data in hand, you can dig a little deeper into why people are buying those all-star products more than the others. After spending a bit of time comparing the features and benefits of those top-selling products to the other items you review on the same page, you can hopefully discover what's making certain things more popular to buy. And once you do that, you can start adding those comparison phrases into your other product descriptions as a way to refer back to the all-star items.

By following this advice, you're uncovering the flaws in those other products and bringing them into the light for your readers, which speeds up their decision making process. It's likely that your visitors would find out those things anyways when they do their own research, so this helps to serve your audience better and to boost sales even more for your top-selling items.

Once I discovered and applied this affiliate content secret, my sales jumped for each of my top 10 list buying guide pages. I couldn't believe that such a simple tweak in my product descriptions could have such a big impact on my earnings. But it did. So use this trick along with the other tips given in the previous few chapters to really squeeze the most out of your top three all-star product recommendations. By doing so, you can hopefully achieve much higher click-through rates and conversions on every affiliate buying guide you write.

SECRET #23

TAKE ADVANTAGE OF CROSS-SELLING

As a full-time affiliate marketer, I'm always looking for ways to increase my earnings from every page I publish. And while the secrets I've shared with you so far in this book are excellent ways to do just that, most of those methods require a bit of time to implement. You have to go through your existing content and think of ways to rewrite those pages to incorporate the lessons learned or think of how you're going to use them well at the start of the writing process.

However, there's actually one trick you can use right now to make more money from each of your existing affiliate pages that doesn't take much time or effort at all to implement; it's called "cross-selling".

Cross-selling is one of my favorite secrets in this book and it's not something I see many other affiliate sites doing, which is a shame. But after you learn what it is and how it can be used, you'll be able to fully maximize your earnings on every affiliate page you publish.

So let's get to it!

WHAT IS CROSS-SELLING?

Cross-selling is a sales technique that businesses use to make more money off of each customer. Traditionally, cross-selling is most often used after a customer has made the decision to buy something from a vendor. With cross-selling, the seller entices the customer to purchase additional upgrades, more expensive items, or other add-ons before the final deal is done. Cross-selling is one of the most powerful ways to increase company profits. It's easier to cross-sell an existing customer who is in an active buying mode than it is to acquire new customers.

The best products for cross-selling are items that are hard to turn down or make logical sense to include along with the purchase.

A classic example of a cross-sell is when you're buying a new car. After you've told the salesperson that you want to buy the car and worked out the payment plan, the salesperson will usually try to add on additional upgrades to make more money on the sale.

Sometimes places like a car dealership will take a loss an initial sale if they know ahead of time that the customer will purchase additional upgrades that will make the company more money in the end. It's a strategic move that some dealerships use to make the customer feel like they're getting an amazing bargain, but in actuality, the dealership is the one who wins.

Here are some examples of cross-selling items that put more money into a car salesperson's pocket during a new car purchase so you can see how this idea works:

- Extended warranty protection
- Lifetime oil changes
- Alloy rims
- Service plan
- Paint protection
- Vehicle tracking device
- Accessories like a tow bar or tinted windows

Car dealerships are not the only place you experience cross-selling as a consumer. You also come across this sales technique in many other industries, such as hotel rentals, insurance carriers, grocery stores, etc. Any business that can encourage you to increase your final bill during the checkout process, like upgrading to a room with a better view, getting a larger life insurance plan, or buying more food in bulk to get a discount, is using the persuasive power of cross-selling to earn more money on the sale.

The truth is that businesses have been using this tactic of cross-selling for hundreds of years because it works. And now you can tap into the same powerful qualities as an affiliate marketer.

HOW YOU CAN USE CROSS-SELLING TO INCREASE YOUR AFFILIATE EARNINGS

The easiest method for using cross-selling on an affiliate page is by including links to accessories and upgrades throughout your product reviews. For example, most of us create top 10 style buying guides of the best products in a particular niche. On those pages, we list the products along with a link to Amazon or some other website to buy them. And that's usually the only way we make a commission.

It's rare that you ever see top 10 style affiliate pages cross-selling other valuable products. And by not doing so, those site owners are missing out on a lot of free earnings.

When I started incorporating this technique of cross-selling into my own affiliate content, I saw an instant lift of 3-5% in earnings on my highest visited pages. And all it took was just recommending a few additional products throughout my reviews.

Using The Strategy

For each product you recommend, add a link in the product description that leads to a common accessory or another item that the user will probably buy at some point in time while owning the item.

A good example of cross-selling so you can see how it works is on a page that reviews printers. All printers require ink to print. So if you were to add in a link to a set of ink cartridges that are compatible with each printer reviewed on the page, then the person who clicks through to buy a printer will most likely also use your affiliate link to purchase the ink. Finding the right ink cartridges for a printer can be a hassle and if you make it easy for the reader to get the right ink, then they'll probably buy the cartridges along with the printer, which will boost your affiliate earnings.

Another good example of cross-selling is a site that reviews chainsaws. Every chainsaw comes with a chain, but that chain will dull over time. So in each product description, you could link to the compatible chain for the reader to buy an extra chain during the checkout process. You could also recommend a chainsaw sharpener, safety gear, and other chainsaw accessories that will make it easier and safer to use the tool. The person who's reading this type of affiliate content is obviously in the buying frame of mind, so why not pile on the options for them to fill their shopping cart and buy everything they need at one time? All it can do is help increase your income as an affiliate marketer.

As you can see, it's really easy to use the power of cross-selling in your affiliate content to make more money. I've been using this tactic myself for years and it's given a major boost to my overall income. I'm really surprised that not many other affiliate marketers have stumbled onto this trick.

But now you have it. So start using it today!

SECRET #24

USE THE POWER OF FLUENCY, FREQUENCY AND EXPOSURE

Have you ever gone into a store to buy something you're not familiar with and were met with multiple brands offering the same item?

If so, how did you choose which product to buy?

If you're like many of us, then you might have gone with your gut instinct. After comparing a few similar items, a lot of us tend to go with the product that *feels* right. We may not know exactly why that is, but something stands out that makes one item seem better than all of the rest. And so we buy it.

For others, they do a quick online search with their smartphone to find reviews of the products they're presented with to get some quick guidance. Then, after seeing that one or two products are being highly rated over and over again by different sites, it becomes much easier to make a decision.

There are also others who just grab the cheapest item on the shelf because they don't want to spend a lot of money on the purchase. They don't think much about it or do any research at all. They just want to pay the lowest cost. And so they do.

Now what you may not know is that there's a secret marketing strategy that popular brands use to influence your decision making process in situations where you don't have any brand attachment. And, unless you just want to buy the cheapest thing out there no matter who makes it, you're likely being influenced by these well-known brands without even knowing it.

There's a reason why brands like Coca-Cola and Nike have their names plastered on so many advertising surfaces and consumer products imaginable. It's also why you see the same brands chasing you with radio advertisements, sponsored social media posts, and other digital content.

While you may try to ignore these brand messages and not click on any of the ads, the real purpose behind this brand strategy has much more to do with your subconscious habits than making a sale on the spot.

Consumer psychology has discovered that there are three powerful ways for a brand to capture a buyer's attention:

- Fluency
- The Mere Exposure Effect
- Frequency Illusion

The short of all of these is that persistence pays off. And you can capitalize on these phenomenons to make more money with your affiliate content. But before I get into the *how to* section of this chapter that can help you boost your affiliate earnings, let's first go over what each of those three psychology concepts means.

FLUENCY

The term fluency can also be thought of as repetition. In psychology, scientists have found that repetition increases processing fluency. What that means is that our brains find repeated words easier to process.

For example, if you've ever heard a new word or met someone with a strange-sounding last name before, then it was probably hard for you to pronounce those things at first. But over time, after you repeated that word or name more and more, it became much easier for you to say. That's a classic example of processing fluency and repetition.

THE MERE EXPOSURE EFFECT

The mere exposure effect is a psychological process by which people tend to develop a preference for things merely because they're familiar with them. When you have repeated exposure to something, you tend to have a more positive attitude toward it.

A good example of this is when one of your favorite bands comes out with a new album. Sometimes bands change their music style and the new album sounds nothing like the previous one. At first, you may not like very many of the songs because you preferred the old style that the band had. But as you listen to those songs more and more, you start to like them. Eventually, you forget that you ever disliked liked them in the first place and adopt the new music style as something you enjoy.

Another common example of the mere exposure effect is when you see someone repeatedly but you've never actually met them before. Even though you've never met, you likely have a positive attitude toward that person because they're familiar to you. Or, at the very least, you have a hidden urge to want to get to know them. This happens a lot in workplaces, grocery stores, gyms, etc., where the same people tend to congregate and repeatedly come back to at the same time throughout the week. As humans, we tend to develop an affinity for the people we routinely see in our communities and throughout our lives.

FREQUENCY ILLUSION

Frequency Illusion is a phenomenon that describes our tendency to see new information, names, ideas, or patterns all around us soon after they're first brought to our attention. Basically, once you encounter something new, you suddenly start noticing it everywhere.

For example, the idea behind frequency illusion happens a lot when people are looking to buy a new car. Once they get their eyes fixed on a particular make and model, they tend to see it everywhere. But before that person wanted that car, they rarely noticed it on the road at all.

Another example of frequency illusion is when you see someone wearing a new style of clothing that you like. Suddenly, it seems like everyone is wearing that brand and now you think that you should too.

However, if you take a step back, you'll actually realize that it's not that everyone is driving the same new car or wearing the same brand of clothes, but it's your senses that are more heightened to those things. Therefore, you're noticing them a lot more even though they may not actually be more popular or present.

TOP BRANDS UNDERSTAND THE POWER OF FLUENCY, FREQUENCY AND EXPOSURE

Now that you know the basics of fluency, frequency, and exposure, you can better understand why brands like Coca-Cola and Nike spend so much money on advertising. It's not that they necessarily expect you to stop what you're doing and go buy one of their products, but rather they want to be at the top of your mind—*or at least subconsciously in the back of it*—when you do make a purchasing decision that's within one of their markets.

If we return to the question I asked at the beginning of this chapter about how you might go about buying a product that you're not familiar with when there are multiple brands offering the same thing, and look at the first two answers, they should now make more sense to you as to why many of us respond in the ways that we do.

In the first instance, people rely on a gut instinct (i.e. a feeling) of what is the right choice to make when they don't have any brand attachment. However, it's highly likely that many of us are making that decision on a subconscious level from advertisements we've seen or heard in the past; even if we're not actively recalling them at that moment.

In the second instance, people who compare products by searching for reviews online are being influenced in many different ways. When we see the same thing being reviewed over and over again, the psychological effects of fluency, frequency, and exposure kick into high gear. Suddenly, those one or two products rise to the top of our decision making pool and all of the other items disappear, even though one of them may actually be a better choice for us.

For brands trying to grow their market share, it's crucial that they heighten their familiarity with consumers on a widespread scale. And the ideas behind frequency, fluency, and exposure are useful ways to get there.

HOW YOU CAN HARNESS THE POWER OF FLUENCY, FREQUENCY AND EXPOSURE

When I first discovered these psychological concepts of frequency, fluency, and exposure, my mind was blown. I couldn't believe that so many of the decisions I've made over the years when I didn't have a brand preference were influenced by them. Now that I look back at some of those decisions, I can definitely tell that these psychological tendencies were at play.

As an affiliate marketer, these phenomenons got me thinking about my affiliate sites and how I could use them for my own benefit. After a lot of brainstorming and testing, I finally figured out a strategy that works. And it's much easier than you may think.

If you look back at chapters #16 and #22, you'll see that I recommended you pick three items to be your all-star products that you focus the most on promoting in your affiliate review guides. Also, you want to continue referring back to those all-star products within the other reviews on the page as a way to increase the desire in your audience for those items.

Now that's just one part of this secret method I developed. If you do nothing else but those two things, then you should still see some gains in your product conversion rates. But if you really want to maximize the sales for those all-star items, then here are two more tricks you'll want to try throughout your affiliate content:

- Use the product name that earns you the most commission more often on the page.
- Scatter additional images of the top three all-star products throughout the page.

I'll expand on these two recommendations further so you can fully understand how to use them and why they work so well to drive up sales. But for now, just know that the best way to increase your profits as an affiliate marketer is to sell more of the item that makes you the most money. And, if you followed my advice from chapter #16, then this product should be your #1 all-star item that you promote.

But how do you get your visitors to want to buy that #1 all-star item more than the other products reviewed on the page?

I'll teach you how to do that next.

USE THE PRODUCT NAME MORE OFTEN

Aside from writing a more persuasive product description for your #1 top all-star item to generate more sales, you can also use the product name more often on the page. As you learned earlier in this chapter, the more fluency, frequency, and exposure someone has with something, the more affinity and positive thoughts they have for that thing.

To capitalize on those psychological processes, just incorporate your #1 all-star product name early on in the affiliate article. Don't wait to mention it in the review section. A good place to start referencing your #1 top pick is in the introduction or right after it. Then, refer to that item again before you actually get to the product review. You can also mention your #2 and #3 all-stars if they make contextual sense in your writing. Finally, repeat the #1 all-star product name one or two more times at the end of your affiliate page so that the person is exposed to it some more.

By the end of your affiliate buying guide, the reader will be so accustomed to seeing that #1 all-star product name that it may get into their subconscious mind. And when they're trying to make a final decision on which product to buy, that item which has had the most fluency just may be the one that *feels* right to them.

EXAMPLES OF REPEATING THE PRODUCT NAME

We'll now look at some examples of how you can incorporate a product name before and after the review section of an affiliate page so you can generate ideas on how to use this strategy in your own content. I'll use several fictitious product names to get the point across. Gentry X12R will be the #1 all-star treadmill. FlexMill B67 will be the #2 all-star product. And Motion NZ3 will be the #3 all-star item.

- In this review, we're going to show you what the top treadmills are for a home gym. As you'll see here, our favorite pick is the Gentry X12R because it offers immersive trainer-led workouts.

Examples Continued...

- When you're looking to buy a treadmill, there are three things you should consider: the physical size, incline height, and track cushioning. The Gentry X12R scores the highest marks in these categories, which is why we ranked it as the best treadmill for home gyms in this guide.
- We spent 15 hours reading through all of the consumer reviews on home gym treadmills and the Gentry X12R kept popping up as the best one to get. It's about the same price as our #3 recommendation, the FlexMill B67, but offers a number of additional features that make it a better choice for the long-term.
- In this section of our review guide, we'll answer some of the top questions people have about treadmills. One popular question people have is, "Are expensive treadmills worth it?" The short answer is yes. There's a big difference between the higher priced treadmills, like the Gentry X12R, and the cheaper alternatives, such as the Motion NZ3. For starters, the mechanism that drives the belt is a crucial element for any high-quality treadmill and the Gentry X12R has one of the best belt systems available.
- We hope you enjoyed this guide on the best treadmills for home gyms. As you discovered, there are a number of good options out there for every person's budget. Regardless if you choose one of our top picks, the Gentry X12R, the FlexMill B67, or the Motion NZ3, or any one of the other seven treadmills reviewed on this page, you'll be getting a great value for your money.

As you can see, this affiliate content writing strategy is not hard to implement. You just need to find unique ways to repeat the name of your top three all-star products throughout the page.

SCATTERING ADDITIONAL IMAGES THROUGH THE POST

The second way that you can use fluency, frequency, and exposure to your advantage is to place images of your top three all-star products throughout the page. This is similar to how we used the product name over and over again to create repetition and familiarity with the item.

The more times a person sees a particular product's image, the more they'll feel like it's a better choice because it's popping up so often. It's kind of like when you find a new pair of shoes that you like, or a new tool, or vacation spot you're interested in. You keep looking at the pictures of it over and over again, and the more you see them, the more attached you get to it. If you don't have enough money to buy it now, then you dream of getting it one day. Or, if you did buy it and it hasn't arrived in the mail yet or the vacation is months away, you keep thinking about how you're going to enjoy the experience as you look at the pictures online.

Images are extremely powerful for making more sales as an affiliate marketer. So if you want to tap into this secret to sell more of your all-star products, then all you have to do is scatter additional images of those products throughout the page. And an easy way to do that for a top ten style buying guide page is to follow this formula:

- Put the #1 all-star product in your featured image for the page. This image appears first and immediately creates a desire for that product in your visitors.
- In the review section, you'll have at least one image for every product you recommend. All products can receive equal visual weight here, or you can add in one or two more pictures of the #1 all-star product to make it stand out.
- After the review section, you should have a buying guide that helps people learn more about how to select a good product for their needs. This is another good area to place an image of your #1 all-star product as the leading picture for this section. Hopefully, you can find an image that shows the product being used by a person. People like to see these types of pictures the best. If not, take your own pictures to include in the content if you already own the item.
- If your word count is long enough in the buying guide section, then layer in images of your #2 and #3 all-star products here as well. That way, the user will see all three of those all-star items again as they scroll down the page. A good method to expand your word count so you can get these pictures included is to answer common questions people have about the products you're reviewing. Then, place the #2 and #3 all-star products pictures next to any one of those questions.

Formula Continued...

- At the end of the affiliate page, you should have a conclusion or a summary of some sort. This is another place where you can add in an image of your #1 all-star product. But if you couldn't fit images of the #2 or #3 all-star products in the previous section of the buying guide, then you may want to consider adding one of those pictures here instead.

As you can see, the #1 all-star product is being featured at least three to four times in a visual format on the page. And while these images are mainly serving as stock photography to help make your content more visually appealing, they're also planting a subconscious desire for the product in your reader's mind.

If you follow both pieces of advice in this chapter on repeating the names of your #1, #2, and #3 all-star products and layering in multiple images of those items throughout the page, your audience will be hit pretty heavy with those items. And the powerful psychological effects of fluency, frequency, and exposure can take over to increase desire and make those products seem like a better choice for many of your readers, which can lead to more instant sales.

SECRET #25

CAPTURE MORE CLICKS WITH IRRESISTIBLE HEADLINES

Did you know that the headline is the most important part of any piece of content? Whether you're writing an affiliate article, newsletter, blog post, sales copy, or email, the headline (or meta title) can often be more essential than the actual content you put on the page.

In fact, numerous studies have been done on how a simple tweak in the words of a headline can boost the click-through rate to a web article by 20% to 50% or more. And those additional clicks can account for thousands of more people visiting a single web page. We see this type of thing in the news and entertainment world all of the time. In those industries, a piece of content lives or dies by the headline that's being used. That's because people scan the headlines to see if a topic interests them or not. If it does grab their attention, then they click. If it doesn't, then they don't.

Some research even indicates that, on average, 8 out of 10 people will read headline copy but only 2 out of 10 will read the rest of the article. Other studies have found that about 60% of people will share a post on social media just by reading the headline. They won't even click through to the site to get the full details of the content to assess the quality of the source.

Talk about the power of headlines!

It's those very reasons why the headline of your affiliate pages is so important. It's also why the headline can determine the effectiveness of the entire piece of content.

Now there has been a lot of good articles written on the power of headlines and how to craft an amazing meta title for general articles, newsletters, blog posts, sales copy, and emails. So I won't be repeating that information here because it's widely available online. All you have to do is search for keyword phrases like "headline tips", "how to write great headlines", or "killer headline examples" to find some good resources on that topic.

What I want to do in this chapter instead is to help you create better headlines (i.e. meta titles) that appear in the search engines to boost the number of clicks that drive traffic to your affiliate pages. The reason this is so crucial is because I see so many affiliate marketers using the same boring meta titles—*and copying each other*—that there's not much variety out there to help one site's page stand out from the rest in the search results. And if you do this same thing, then it can cause your affiliate pages to perform poorly without you even knowing it.

EXAMPLES OF COMMON (AND BORING) META TITLES

Below is an example of what I mean by boring and copycat meta titles. At the time of this writing, I did a keyword search for "best ceramic heaters" and these were the top ten page titles that appeared on Google:

1. 9 Best Ceramic Heaters (Reviews and Buying Guide for 2020)
2. 8 Best Ceramic Heaters Reviewed in Detail (2020)
3. The Best Ceramic Space Heaters for 2020
4. Best Ceramic Space Heaters 2020 (Top Picks & Reviews)
5. Best Ceramic Heater Reviews (Buying Guide 2020)
6. Top 5 Best Ceramic Heater Reviews and Buying Guide for 2020
7. 10 Best Ceramic Heaters (Reviews & Buying Guide for 2020)
8. The 9 Best Ceramic Space Heaters
9. The Best Ceramic Space Heaters (2020 Buyers Guide)
10. 15 Best Ceramic Space Heaters for 2020

Now suppose you were the person who was doing research to find the best ceramic heater for their home. Which of those pages would you click on?

If you're like most people, then you'll have a hard time deciding on which of those pages to visit because all of the titles have similar language. There's nothing unique that sets them apart. The only noticeable difference is that some of those meta titles include a number that represents how many ceramic heaters are reviewed on the page, like 9, 10, or 15. But would a casual visitor be more attracted to the 9 best ceramic heaters page, the 10 best ceramic heaters page, or the 15 best ceramic heaters page? Or, would they click on all of those pages in order to find out why one site only lists 9 products while the others list 10 and 15 best ceramic heaters?

Do you see how confusing that can be for the average consumer?

If you weren't privy to this already, the reason all of these top ranking affiliate pages have similar meta titles is because they're trying to maximize the search engine optimization (SEO) for their content. To rank high for the keyword phrase "best ceramic heaters", you have to have it in your meta title. Additionally, many of these site owners also want their page to rank for the phrase "ceramic heater reviews" and so they have the word "reviews" in the meta title as well. The year "2020" is also included as a way to make the article seem fresh and relevant to the searcher.

While combining all of those target keywords into a meta title is great for SEO and ranking purposes, it can be bad for the consumers who are doing the searching because there's nothing unique about any of those page titles to capture the person's attention. And even more importantly, their click.

Now with all the being said, there's a lot we can learn from the news and entertainment industry and how big media companies use headlines to grab people's attention, get more of their articles read, and have them shared on social media. And if you apply the tips I'm about to share with you next, then you can hopefully make your headlines (i.e. meta titles) stand out from your competitors in the search engines so you can boost your affiliate page clicks to get more traffic.

HOW TO WRITE MORE ATTENTION GRABBING META TITLES

There are five simple tricks you can use to spice up the meta titles on your affiliate pages in order to capture more clicks and still hit your core SEO keywords to get higher rankings. As you'll discover next, these strategies for writing meta titles can make your affiliate pages seem much more interesting to read and can entice people to visit your pages over the competition.

1. Use the Element of Surprise

People love novelty, and meta titles that surprise people are a good way to get more clicks. Unpredictable things turn on the pleasure centers in our brains and heighten our interests. Thus, surprises can be far more stimulating and grab our attention much better than the normal run-of-the-mill things that you come across, like the top ten best ceramic heater headlines I showed you previously.

Here are some examples of headlines that include the element of surprise:

- The 10 Best Ceramic Heaters That'll Keep Your Butt Warm All Winter Long
- The Best Ceramic Heaters, according to a cold-natured Grandma
- Best Ceramic Heater Reviews (For Frugal Eyes Only) 2020 Buying Guide
- 10 Best Ceramic Heaters for Christmas That are Santa-Approved
- The 9 Best Ceramic Heaters That Fit in the Palm of Your Hand

2. Ask a Question

Questions naturally prime our curiosity, and people always want to know the answer that's on the other side of a question. We can't stand the unknown. So the best questions to use in your meta titles are ones that are about something your readers can relate to or want to know about. By following this strategy, you can tempt people to click on your affiliate page's link in order to cure their wonder.

Here are some examples of using questions in headlines:

- What are the Best Ceramic Heaters? Our Guide Reviews the Top 2020 Models
- Are These the Best Ceramic Heaters? Our Expert Reviews Tell the Whole Story
- Looking for the Best Ceramic Heaters? Our 2020 Review Has Some Surprising Comparisons
- Which of These 5 Best Ceramic Heaters Would You Choose for Your Home or Office?
- What Do the 9 Best Ceramic Heaters All Have in Common? Our 2020 Review Has the Answer

3. Create Curiosity

A curiosity gap is the discrepancy between what we currently know and what we want to know. Once a person knows a little bit about something, they'll then want to find out more so they can fill in the missing information. By making your meta titles intriguing, but incomplete, you can provoke people to click on your affiliate page's links to close that curiosity gap.

Here are some examples of creating curiosity in headlines:

- The 10 Best Ceramic Heaters of All Time (#2 is On Sale Now)
- 9 Best Ceramic Heaters That Cost Pennies to Use (2020 Reviews)
- The Best & Worst Ceramic Heaters for 2020, According to Top Experts
- These 10 Best Ceramic Heaters Cost Less Than $80! (Reviews for 2020)
- 5 Best Ceramic Heaters for a Poor College Student (Frugal Reviews for 2020)

4. Use Negative Words

Although you must have the word "best" or "top" in your affiliate page's meta title to rank for those types of keywords in the search engines, you can also attract people to visit your page by adding negative words to the headline. Negative words are unexpected and tap into the human desire to avoid pain or loss. If you include words like "stop", "don't", "avoid", "not", "never", or "mistake", you can use people's insecurities against them to gain more clicks—*and traffic*—for your affiliate pages.

Here are some examples of how negative words can work in headlines:

- The 10 Best Ceramic Heaters and Which 5 to Avoid (Reviews for 2020)
- The Best Ceramic Heaters are NOT What You Think (Details Inside)
- 9 Best Ceramic Heaters That Will Never Go Out of Style
- STOP! Don't Let These 15 Best Ceramic Heaters Pass You By
- 10 Best Ceramic Heaters for 2020 (Plus 2 That Are a Big Mistake for Anyone to Buy)

5. Refer to Your Audience

In chapter #3 of this book, you learned about how to use the 2nd person pronouns "you" and "your" to subconsciously draw your readers into the text and feel like the content was written personally for them. By applying that same trick to your meta titles—*and referring to your audience*—you can make people think, "That's for me!", when they come across your affiliate page's headline in the search engines. And that feeling can entice more people to want to click on it.

Here are some examples of referring to the audience in headlines:

- Best Ceramic Heaters: Your Ultimate Guide with Expert Reviews
- 10 Best Ceramic Heaters That Fit Your Budget & Style for 2020
- 9 Best Ceramic Heaters You Can Carry With You Around the House (2020 Reviews)

Examples Continued...

- 15 Best Ceramic Heaters for Your Home or Apartment, According to Experts
- The 9 Best Ceramic Heaters You've Never Seen Before (2020 Reviews)

TEST MULTIPLE META TITLES

The last piece of advice I want to give you before we end this chapter is to always be testing your meta titles. What might seem like a great meta title for an affiliate page at first might not capture as many clicks as you thought, and vice versa. In my experience, sometimes the meta titles that I thought were weak actually outperformed the ones that were stronger. Therefore, it's best to come up with several versions of meta titles for each of your affiliate pages and test them against each other. Over time, you'll find out which meta title increases your clicks the most from the search engines and then you can keep that one intact.

Additionally, if after a few months you notice that an affiliate page is not getting as many clicks as it did previously, then go to Google and check the meta titles of your competitors. Perhaps those site owners have changed their meta titles to entice more clicks from the searchers or Google may be favoring a different type of meta title structure. By doing a quick keyword search and analysis, you can compare your affiliate page's meta title to what's ranking on the first page of Google and make the necessary adjustments.

SECTION 2

AFFILIATE PAGE STRUCTURE SECRETS

In this section, I'll teach you how to properly structure an affiliate buying guide page that not only produces better click-through rates and conversions but also has a better chance at ranking higher in Google. I'm literally giving away all of my secret on page structures and keyword placements that have helped me dominate various niches and make more money with my affiliate sites.

In the beginning of my affiliate marketing career, I didn't have any clue on how to structure an affiliate buying guide or where to place my target keywords. Just the fact that I was making sales was exciting. Page structure and keyword placement were the furthest things from my mind. However, once I decided to get serious about making affiliate marketing the main source for my full-time income, I knew I had to learn more about conversion rate optimization and on-page SEO tactics. So I spent a lot of time talking with other affiliate marketers to find out how they were structuring their content and using target keywords on the page. But what I learned was that many of my peers didn't have a dedicated formula in place for how to craft a winning affiliate buying guide. Instead, they just copied what the other top ranking sites were doing without knowing why the site owner structured their page in a certain way. And while that method can work to generate some sales, it doesn't give you a solid foundation behind the principles for what makes a successful affiliate page. Therefore, if you do that too, then you're blindly copying the top ranking sites with the hope that they know what they're doing to make money online.

But here's the truth, many of the top ranking affiliate pages are not structured 100% correctly. Sure, those pages may have some of the attributes in place that I'll share with you in this section but the organization of the content and the placement of keywords is not being maximized to their full potential. And that can lead to lower affiliate earnings because the content is not meeting the needs of a large percentage of their visitors.

Therefore, I decided to include the information in this section of the book to help you bypass all of the guesswork on how to structure a good affiliate buying guide. Like the first part of this book, it took me many years of trial and error to establish the guiding principles that I'm going to share with you here. I didn't just come up with this framework overnight. I fine-tuned and tweaked my affiliate page structures and keyword placements on hundreds of pages before I finally discovered what worked the best. I now follow two simple formulas on every affiliate buying guide I publish to generate the most income from them. And now you can too.

WHY ARE THERE TWO AFFILIATE PAGE STRUCTURES?

Over the years, I've learned an important lesson in affiliate marketing: *what works well for one niche might not work well for another*.

What I mean by this is that consumer psychology in every market is different. In some niches, and even particular products in those spaces, consumers prefer to have the buying guide and review information structured in a certain way. For example, a person who's searching for the best table saw has a different frame of mind than someone who wants to find the best weight loss program. And if you deliver the right page structure for each of those types of audiences, then you can improve your affiliate sales.

I used to think that I could just create one boiler plate template to follow for all of my affiliate buying guides; however, after a lot of testing, I discovered that I was leaving a lot of money on the table by operating with that frame of mind. Once I started testing different page structures against each other, I found out that certain types of affiliate content made more earnings if I used one type of page structure over another.

Eventually, I narrowed it down to two affiliate page structures and keyword formulas that work well for most niches. And so I stick with these on every affiliate site I own because they work so well.

In the next two chapters, you'll discover what those two affiliate page structures are and how they can help you create a higher-earning affiliate buying guide, which is a list-style post that promotes between five to ten products. If you're creating an affiliate page like *The Top 10 Best Baby Strollers* or *8 Best Rifle Scopes for Deer Hunters*, then these structures can work well to generate higher click-through rates and conversions for the products you review and hopefully rank the page higher in Google for your target keywords.

My best advice for which page structure you should choose for your affiliate content is to create both types of pages and split test them against each other. That way, you can know for sure which structure works best for each one of your affiliate pages. You'd be surprised at how one structure may deliver much better results over the other for each affiliate buying guide you publish. On my affiliate sites, I have both page structures in place and each buying guide uses the version that generates the most sales. If you don't have the ability to do split testing right now, then just choose the page structure you like best. Either option will work better than just structuring your affiliate pages without following a proven framework.

SECRET PAGE STRUCTURE #1

The affiliate page structure you'll learn here is my go-to format that always works for top 10 style buying guides. There's nothing too fancy about it either that requires special coding skills or plugins. If you have a plain text editor, like the one in WordPress, then you can easily format your own affiliate buying guides to match this template.

Due to the physical size limitations of this book, I couldn't include the full page example here. But starting on the next page, I will explain what each of the important sections are that make up this page structure and tell you where to include your target keyword throughout the content to help improve its rankings.

Meta Title

The meta title is not a visual page structure element that the visitor sees, but it is the text that appears in the search engines as the title for your affiliate page. You want to place your target keyword in the meta title because it has a lot of SEO value and weight for rankings.

Meta Description

The meta description is another important aspect for ranking purposes that's not a visual on-page element. Many people argue that the meta description has zero SEO weight, but I include the target keyword here anyways. You never know if Google might give some value to this field in the future, so it's good to incorporate your target keyword into this short description for the page. Plus, Google will often pull the meta description to show for your page in the search results and it'll bold the target keyword that a user searched. This attribute can help entice more people to click on your page's link.

H1 Page Title

The H1 tag is the first visual on-page element that contributes to your page structure. The title for your affiliate page should include your target keyword and be wrapped in an H1 tag because it has a lot of weight for SEO rankings. The H1 page title doesn't have to be the same as the meta title; however, it's good to make them similar. For example, if you were targeting the keyword "best table saws", then the meta title could be "Top 10 Best Table Saws for 2020 (Buying Guide & Reviews)" while the H1 tag is "Top 10 Best Table Saws (Buying Guide & Reviews)".

Introduction with an Image

The introduction is an extremely important part of your affiliate content and page structure. It can make or break how many people actually stay on your page as well as how high your page ranks in Google. The purpose of the introduction is to hook your visitor into the content and persuade them to want to read more. If you don't do that, then the person will likely bounce from the page.

You want to keep your introductions short: around 150 to 200 words. You don't want people spending a lot of time here, but rather encourage them to keep reading so they get into the meat of your affiliate content.

The introduction is also a good location to put your target keyword to help improve your affiliate page's rankings. Some SEO case studies show that having your keyword within the first 100 words can help give your page a slight ranking boost. So add it within the first two to three sentences to get the most benefit.

Additionally, you want to have an image alongside your page's introduction. The image can be located above the text or right justified with the text wrapping around it. A good trick here is to include an image that features your #1 all-star product as mentioned in chapter #24. You also want to put your target keyword in the image filename and ALT tag. For example, if you're targeting the keyword "best table saws", then you'll want the image filename to be "best-table-saws.jpg" and the image ALT tag to be alt="Best Table Saws" to get the most SEO ranking value.

H2 List Title

After the introduction, you want to immediately jump into your product review list. People who are actively looking for helpful product review content are usually in an active buying mode, so they really just want to know what the top models are to choose between. Therefore, you want to give your visitors exactly what they're looking for as quickly as possible on the page.

Use an H2 tag to kick off the product reviews list and insert your target keyword here. For example, if it were targeting the keyword "best table saws", then it could be "Best Table Saws List" or "Best Table Saw Reviews". Having an H2 tag located high on the page with the full version of the keyword can help to establish SEO relevance.

(The next three page structure elements are what make up the bulk of each individual product review, which you'll repeat for every item reviewed on the page.)

H3 Product Name

All of the products you review on your affiliate page should start with an H3 tag. The H3 tag will include the number that the item ranks on the list and the product name. For example, "1. Acme PC713 Table Saw" or "2. RedMax X187 Table Saw".

It's important to include the basic version of your target keyword in each of the product names. For example, if you were targeting a page on the best table saws, then you'd want each H3 product name to include the word "Table Saw" in it. Don't just copy and paste the product name as it's listed on the merchant's website. Sometimes these product names don't include the target keyword you're trying to rank the affiliate page for. For example, a table saw might be listed as "RedMax X187 Saw" on a merchant's website. That name doesn't have the word "Table" in it. Therefore, you'd want to change the product name to be "RedMax X187 Table Saw" on your affiliate page so it does have the full word "Table Saw" in it.

Finally, you also want to make the H3 product names clickable with your affiliate link.

Product Description with an Image

Below the product name wrapped in an H3 tag is where you'll provide the written review of the product. This information is in plain text without any special HTML markup. Write between 200 to 400 words for each product review.

Include your target keyword in the first product description. An easy way to do that is to place it within the first sentence or last sentence of the review. For example, if you were targeting the keyword "best table saw", then you could start the first product review like this:

- If you're looking for the best table saw money can buy, this is it.

Or, you could end the first product review like this:

- As you can see, this really is the best table saw that's available.

You also want to have at least one image of the product included here so the visitor can see what it looks like. The image can be located above the text description or right justified with the text wrapping around it.

Finally, the image for each product should be clickable with your affiliate link.

Check Price Button

At the end of each product review description there should be a button for the reader to click on to check the price of the item. Essentially, this is your call-to-action (CTA) to entice people to visit the product's sales page so they can buy it. Not everyone will click on the product name wrapped in an H3 tag or the image, so it's good to have a CTA button like this after you've finished your written review of the product.

I've tested many variations of the words used in this CTA button and "Check Price" has always delivered the highest click-through rates and conversions. It outperformed "Buy Now", "Add to Cart", "See Reviews" and other similar CTAs.

You can do your own testing to see if the results are the same or just stick with what has been proven to work by using "Check Price" on your CTA button.

(The last three elements we covered should be repeated for each individual product review on the page. Just remember to change the number in the H3 product name to the appropriate position in the list. The next item in the list would be 2., followed by 3., and so on.)

H2 Buying Guide Section

After you're done reviewing all of the products in your list, you'll then move into the buying guide section of the page. This section is for people who need more information to help them make a purchasing decision. Perhaps they're not sure how to tell the difference between two competing products or what certain features mean. This section will help educate your visitors on the various things that pertain to the items being reviewed so they can make a final choice.

Use an H2 tag to start the buying guide section and insert your target keyword here. If you're targeting a keyword that has the word "best" in it, then don't include the word "best" in this H2 tag. For example, if you were targeting the keyword "best table saws", then you could label the H2 element as "Table Saw Buying Guide" or "Buying Guide for Table Saws". Having an additional H2 tag on the page with the basic version of the keyword can help to establish SEO relevance without being overoptimized.

H3 Feature to Consider

The first part of the buying guide section should include the various features that are worth considering which relate to the products you're reviewing.

Use an H3 tag for the name of each feature and include as many as you need to fully educate your readers on the topic. For example, if you were reviewing table saws, then you could include features like "Blade Cutting Size", "Stand Height", "Maximum Cutting Width", "Dust Collection System", etc. And each of those feature names would be wrapped in an H3 tag.

Feature Description

Below the H3 for each feature to consider is where you'll provide an explanation for that feature.

This information is in plain text without any special HTML markup. Write as many words as you'd like here. The purpose is to describe what the feature is and why it's important for the reader to take into consideration. The more you can inform your audience here, the less likely they'll go to another site for additional research.

(Repeat the last two elements for each feature to consider.)

H2 Questions and Answers Section

After you discuss the various features to consider, you'll then want to answer common questions people have about the types of products you're reviewing.

Use an H2 tag to start this section of the buying guide and insert your target keyword here. If you're targeting a keyword that has the word "best" in it, then don't include the word "best" in this H2 tag. For example, if you're targeting the keyword "best table saws", then label the H2 as "Common Questions About Tables Saws", "Frequently Asked Questions About Table Saws", or "FAQs for Table Saws". Having another H2 tag on the page with the basic version of the keyword can help to establish SEO relevance without being overoptimized.

H3 Question Title

This is simply the title of the question you're going to answer.

Use an H3 tag for each question title. A good way to generate ideas for the types of questions to include here can be taken from Google. Just do a search for your target keyword and you'll see a "People Also Ask" box on the search results page. These are questions that people are actively searching for that relate to your keyword. So put as many of these related questions as you can on the page. For example, if you were targeting the keyword "best table saws", then these are a few good questions that could be included which appeared in Google's People Also Ask box: "What is the Best Table Saw for Woodworking?", "What is the Best Table Saw for Beginners?", and "How Dangerous are Table Saws?"

Answer to the Question

Below the H3 tag for each question title is where you'll provide an answer for each question. This information is in plain text without any special HTML markup. Write as many words as you'd like here. The purpose is to give a clear enough answer so that your audience won't want to go to another site for additional research.

(Repeat the last two elements for each question and answer. There is no limit to how many questions you should answer here.)

H2 Helpful Tips Section

After you're done with the questions and answers, you'll then want to provide a section with helpful tips for your readers. The purpose of this section is to encourage your visitors to start thinking about actually using the products in the best possible way. This subtle trick can work to influence people to make an immediate purchase because they're already getting mentally involved with using the product. So try to think of general tips that can apply to every one of the products reviewed on the page to include here.

Use an H2 tag for this section of the buying guide and insert your target keyword here. If you're targeting a keyword that has the word "best" in it, then don't include the word "best" in this H2 tag. For example, if you were targeting the keyword "best table saws", then label the H2 as "Tips On Using Your New Table Saw" or "Helpful Table Saw Tips". Having another H2 tag on the page with the basic version of the keyword can help to establish SEO relevance without being overoptimized.

Bullet Point List of Tips

Below the H2 tag is where you'll provide a list of tips in bullet point fashion. Begin each item in the list with a bolded word or short phrase. Then describe the tip in plain text. List as many tips as you can here. The more value you can provide your readers within this section of the buying guide, the better your chances are at making a sale. If a reader is well-equipped to use a product before they've even bought it, then the easier it'll be for them to make a purchase.

Here's an example tip for an affiliate page that reviews table saws and the format you should follow for each tip in the bullet list:

- **Use a Push Stick:** If you're cutting a thin piece of wood that puts your hand within one foot of the table saw blade, then it's time to reach for a push stick. This is a long notched stick that you use to hook over the end of the board to push it on through the cut while keeping your hands safely away from the blade. You can make your own or buy one that's specially made for this purpose.

H2 Summary

This is the final section of your affiliate page. It basically summarizes everything that the person learned throughout the content. It's also a good place to put your target keyword.

Use an H2 tag for this section and insert your full target keyword here. For example, if you were targeting the keyword "best table saws", then label the H2 as "Wrap Up on the Best Table Saws" or "Best Table Saws Summary". Having an additional H2 tag on the page with the full target keyword can help to establish SEO relevance.

Summary Description with an Image

Below the H2 tag for the summary is where you'll provide a short conclusion for the page.

This information is in plain text without any special HTML markup. It should be between 150 to 200 words. You also want to place your target keyword here. Some SEO case studies show that having your keyword within the last 100 words can help give your page a slight ranking boost. So add it into the last sentence or two.

You also want to have an image in this section. The image can be located above the summary description or right justified with the text wrapping around it. A good choice to use here is to include an image that features your #1 all-star product as mentioned in chapter #24.

Additionally, if you're targeting more than one target keyword on the page, then you can insert that keyword into this image filename and ALT text. For example, if you were targeting the keywords "best table saws" and "table saw reviews", and the first image on the page with the introduction has "best-table-saw.jpg" for the filename and alt="Best Table Saw", then you could make this image's file name "table-saw-reviews.jpg" and the ALT tag be alt="Table Saw Reviews Summary".

RECAP ON WHERE TO PLACE YOUR TARGET KEYWORD

There's much debate in the SEO community on keyword density and proper placement of your target keyword for maximum on-page SEO value. But after years of testing, I've found that my affiliate pages always rank well when I include my target keyword in the locations mentioned in this affiliate page structure template.

On the next page, you'll find a recap for those keyword locations. The purpose is to give you a quick checklist to follow when you're writing your own affiliate buying guides.

This checklist for *Secret Page Structure #1* assumes that you're targeting a keyword with the word "best" in it.

- Meta Title (with the word "best" included)
- Meta Description (with the word "best" included)
- H1 Page Title (with the word "best" included)
- Introduction (with the word "best" included within the first 100 words)
- Image filename for the first image on the page (with the word "best" included)
- Image ALT tag for the first image on the page (with the word "best" included)
- H2 List Title (with the word "best" included)
- H3 Product Names (without the word "best")
- Product description for the first product reviewed on the page (with the word "best" included in the first or last sentence)
- H2 Buying Guide Section (without the word "best")
- H2 Questions and Answers Section (without the word "best")
- H2 Helpful Tips Section (without the word "best")
- H2 Summary (with the word "best" included)
- Summary description (with the word "best" included within the last 100 words on the page)

Note: Google's ranking algorithm is always changing, so these keyword locations are not set in stone and cannot guarantee that your page will rank higher by using them. However, I've been using this same keyword formula on every page I publish with success. So hopefully, these locations can work for you too. But it's always good to do your own testing.

SECRET PAGE STRUCTURE #2

This is another affiliate page structure you can try. It includes most of the same elements as *Secret Page Structure #1* but with a few additional sections and a different order. You'll also need some coding skills or a plugin to create the comparison table that's referenced here.

This *Secret Page Structure #2* basically adds a comparison table after the introduction and then launches into the *Features to Consider* section of the buying guide. After that comes the product reviews list, followed by the questions and answers, and the helpful tips sections. The page then ends with a summary.

This affiliate page structure is good for niches where people need a bit more education before they feel comfortable making a purchase, such as high-priced items that take more mental processing before a final decision is made.

As with *Secret Page Structure #1*, I couldn't include a full page example of this structure here because of the physical size limitations of this book. But I can explain what each of the important sections are that make up this page structure and tell you where to include your target keyword throughout the content to help improve its rankings.

In order to keep things brief; however, I won't repeat the explanations for elements that overlap between *Secret Page Structure #1*. For a recap on any of those sections, just flip back to the previous chapter of the book.

Meta Title

(Same advice as *Secret Page Structure #1*)

Meta Description

(Same advice as *Secret Page Structure #1*)

H1 Page Title

(Same advice as *Secret Page Structure #1*)

Introduction with an Image

(Same advice as *Secret Page Structure #1*)

H2 Comparison Chart

This section provides a table that allows your readers to quickly compare each product side-by-side that's reviewed on the page. Some of your visitors will use this table to make a quick buying decision.

Use an H2 tag to start this comparison table section and insert your target keyword here. For example, if you were targeting the keyword "best table saws", then it could be something like "Best Table Saws Comparison Chart" or "Compare the Best Table Saws". Having an H2 tag located high on the page with the full version of the keyword can help to establish SEO relevance.

Comparison Table

This is the actual table with the comparison information for each product reviewed on the page. My conversion rate optimization tests have shown that all you need is a three column table that includes a few simple elements, as you'll see on the next page.

- Column 1: Product Image
- Column 2: Product Details
- Column 3: Check Price Button

Columns 1 and 3 are self-explanatory. Just remember to make both of these items clickable with your affiliate link. For column 2, you'll want to include the product name (with your affiliate link attached) and a bullet point list with 3-5 features/benefits. All of the features/benefits should be within the same category for each product so that people can easily compare them to each other. The first item in your bullet point lists should be bold and give a short reason for why that product stands out against the others.

Here's an example of a comparison table for an affiliate buying guide that's targeting the keyword "best table saws". I only included the first three products in the table for brevity's sake.

Image	Product Details	Price
	Acme Table Saw Xl38 • **Best overall table saw** • 12-inch blade • 99% wood dust collection • Comes with a stand	CHECK PRICE
	Piper Table Saw 100 • **Cheapest table saw** • 8 1/4-inch blade • No wood dust collection • No stand included	CHECK PRICE
	Saw Buster Table 708668 • **Good value table saw** • 10-inch blade • 80% wood dust collection • Optional stand available	CHECK PRICE

H2 Buying Guide Section

(Same advice as *Secret Page Structure #1*)

H3 Feature to Consider

(Same advice as *Secret Page Structure #1*)

Feature Description

(Same advice as *Secret Page Structure #1*)

(Repeat the last two elements for each feature to consider.)

H2 List Title

(Same advice as *Secret Page Structure #1*)

H3 Product Name

(Same advice as *Secret Page Structure #1*)

Product Description with an Image

(Same advice as *Secret Page Structure #1*)

Check Price Button

(Same advice as *Secret Page Structure #1*)

(The last three elements we covered should be repeated for each individual product review on the page. Just remember to change the number in the H3 product name to the appropriate position in the list. The next item in the list would be 2., followed by 3., and so on.)

H2 Questions and Answers Section

(Same advice as *Secret Page Structure #1*)

H3 Question Title

(Same advice as *Secret Page Structure #1*)

Answer to the Question

(Same advice as *Secret Page Structure #1*)

(Repeat the last two elements for each question and answer. There is no limit to how many questions you should answer here.)

H2 Helpful Tips Section

(Same advice as *Secret Page Structure #1*)

Bullet Point List with Tips

(Same advice as *Secret Page Structure #1*)

H2 Summary

(Same advice as *Secret Page Structure #1*)

Summary Description with an Image

(Same advice as *Secret Page Structure #1*)

RECAP ON WHERE TO PLACE YOUR TARGET KEYWORD

As mentioned in the recap for *Secret Page Structure #1*, there are certain locations on the page that have helped my affiliate pages rank better when I include my target keyword in them.

But because Google's ranking algorithm is always changing, these keyword locations are not set in stone and cannot guarantee that your page will rank higher by using them. However, I've been using this same keyword formula on every page I publish with success. So hopefully, these locations can work for you too. But it's always good to do your own testing.

On the next page, you'll find a recap for those keyword locations. The purpose is to give you a quick checklist to follow when you're writing your own affiliate buying guides.

This checklist for *Secret Page Structure #2* assumes that you're targeting a keyword with the word "best" in it.

- Meta Title (with the word "best" included)
- Meta Description (with the word "best" included)
- H1 Page Title (with the word "best" included)
- Introduction (with the word "best" included within the first 100 words)
- Image filename for the first image on the page (with the word "best" included)
- Image ALT tag for the first image on the page (with the word "best" included)
- H2 Comparison Chart (with the word "best" included)
- H2 Buying Guide Section (without the word "best")
- H2 List Title (with the word "best" included)
- H3 Product Names (without the word "best")
- Product description for the first product reviewed on the page (with the word "best" included in the first or last sentence)
- H2 Questions and Answers Section (without the word "best")
- H2 Helpful Tips Section (without the word "best")
- H2 Summary (with the word "best" included)
- Summary description (with the word "best" included within the last 100 words on the page)

CONCLUSION

Congratulations! You made it to the end of the book.

Now I bet your head is swimming with tons of ideas for how to improve your affiliate content and maximize your earnings.

We covered a lot within these pages, but just remember that the secrets I've shared with you on how to boost your reader engagement and affiliate earnings took me more than 10 years to discover. There was a lot of research and testing that ultimately led to these affiliate content writing strategies and page structure layouts. So don't feel like you have to go out and immediately change everything on your affiliate pages today. It's fine to take it slow and pick the tactics that you feel like you can implement quickly and then work on incorporating the rest.

If there's one thing I've learned during my journey in affiliate marketing, it's that you have to be patient. Building a successful business like this is a marathon, not a sprint.

However, by following the methods outlined in this book, you can bypass the many years of trial and error that it takes to find out what actually works to improve the click-through rates and conversions of the products you promote on your affiliate site. And that can help you to experience faster results.

All of the secrets you learned in this book are the same tactics I use on my own affiliate sites to make them more profitable. And you now have those same secrets to use for your own benefit.

Let's quickly recap what those secrets are:

Secret #1: Identify your target buyer persona. Craft your content so that it speaks to a specific set of visitors.

Secret #2: Use 1st person singular pronouns to act like an authority in your niche. Those are "I", "me", "my", and "mine". People want to hear the thoughts and opinions of others who have firsthand experience with things.

Secret #3: Use 2nd person pronouns to write directly to your readers. Those are "you" and "your". These two little words can help your readers better connect the points in your copy to their own lives.

Secret #4: Use 1st person plural pronouns to bond with your audience. Those are "we", "us", and "our". Writing in this way can trigger a subconscious response in your readers by bringing people into the emotional context of your statements and transferring your thoughts and opinions onto them.

Secret #5: Choose active voice over passive voice. Active voice makes your content much more clear and concise, which also makes it easier to understand and for people to relate to.

Secret #6: Use power words. Those are words like "trust", "easy", "powerful", "best", and "one-of-a-kind". By using these types of power words in your affiliate content, you can make your products seem irresistible to your readers.

Secret #7: Write like a 7th grader, or even like a 3rd grader. The easier your content is to read, the wider your audience becomes. And the more people who can grasp your message, the more sales you can make from the products you promote.

Secret #8: Use one sentence paragraphs, or at most two. Long blocks of text are hard to read, especially on mobile devices. Also, people like to skim as they read online. So break up your sentences into one or two line paragraphs so the content is easier to digest.

Secret #9: Vary your sentence length. Creating rhythm with your words makes your affiliate content more engaging for your visitors to read and keeps them on the page longer.

Secret #10: Ask rhetorical questions. Rhetorical questions help to engage your readers and persuade them to consider the comments and suggestions you make on your affiliate pages more deeply.

Secret #11: Use expert words. Those are words like "proven", "test", "research", and "expert". By using these types of words on your affiliate pages, you can make your content seem more trustworthy and credible.

Secret #12: Quote someone. Many people are easily persuaded by the testimonials and quotes from other individuals. So try to add at least two or more quotes in every affiliate page you publish. You can get quotes in three ways: 1) by reaching out to an industry expert, 2) asking someone inside your company to provide one, or 3) quoting yourself.

Secret #13: Label your readers with a noun. You can create a stronger affiliation with your audience if you label them with a catchy noun. By labeling your readers with a term that they self-identify with, you can make your content seem more relatable and connect better with them.

Secret #14: Bait your readers with a hook. The introduction is the most important part of your affiliate page. If you don't entice the visitor to keep reading, then they'll likely leave. You can instantly hook your readers by starting the introduction with a question, an interesting fact, or an anecdote.

Secret #15: Push your visitors to read more. As humans, we have a strong desire for closure. That's why open loops can be so powerful in your writing. Use open loops to spark curiosity in your readers but don't deliver the answers right away. This keeps your audience engaged and scrolling through the page. And the more time a person spends on your content, the more likely they are to buy something.

Secret #16: Pick three products to be your all-stars. These three products will be the ones that you focus the most on getting your visitors to buy. A good framework for these all-star items include:

- #1 should be the most expensive item with the most features.
- #2 should be the least expensive item with the best features.
- #3 should be an item with a moderate price and a moderate set of features that offers a good overall value.

Secret #17: Apply the feature stacking trick. Consumer psychologists have discovered that people perceive a product with a long list of features to be more valuable. Therefore, it's best to list out as many features as possible for your top three all-star picks. Then, list fewer features as you go down the list for the other products reviewed on the page as a way to make them less attractive.

Secret #18: Focus on the person, not the product. People buy products that solve their problems, not because they have a great set of features. Add a benefit statement for every feature you highlight in your product reviews. That way, the reader can get a better sense of how a product's features will improve their life.

Secret #19: Always start with the strongest benefits. People tend to remember the first piece of information they encounter better than the material presented later in a sequence. And the first things we come across set the standard for everything else that follows. So lead each product description with the strongest benefits.

Secret #20: Keep your negatives brief, but do include them. Having at least one negative aspect for each product you review adds authenticity to your affiliate content. But don't go overboard on the negativity. Otherwise, you'll deter people from buying the products you promote. You can also add a positive statement after each negative comment as a way to re-frame it.

Secret #21: If you give a strong why, more people will buy. There are ten general reasons why people buy things:

1. To save time
2. To save money
3. To make money
4. To avoid effort
5. To escape pain
6. To gain comfort
7. To get praise
8. To feel loved
9. To improve health
10. To increase social status

If a person feels like they can gain or avoid an internal desire by getting one of the products you recommend, then it will lower their resistance to making an immediate purchase. Therefore, you should include one or more statements in each of your product reviews that aligns with the top reasons for why people buy things.

Secret #22: Keep referring back to your all-stars. Your goal as an affiliate marketer is to make it easier for your visitors to make a buying decision. By constantly referring back to your top three all-star items within the other product reviews, you can persuade your readers that one of those top three picks is better suited for their needs, and hopefully make an immediate purchase.

Secret #23: Take advantage of cross-selling. You can easily boost your affiliate earnings by adding links to other popular accessories and upgrades in each product description. For example, all printers need ink, so you can add a link to the ink cartridge for every product reviewed on the page as a way to make more money from each visitor.

Secret #24: Use the power of fluency, frequency, and exposure. The more times someone is exposed to a product, the more they'll feel like it's the right choice. You can tap into several powerful psychology phenomenons by repeating the names of your top all-star products throughout the page and by adding multiple pictures of them.

Secret #25: Capture more clicks with irresistible headlines. You can entice more people to click on your affiliate pages in the search results by making the meta titles stand out from the competition. Use one of these five tricks:

1. Use the Element of Surprise
2. Ask a Question
3. Create Curiosity
4. Use Negative Words
5. Refer to Your Audience

Secret Page Structures #1 and #2: By structuring your affiliate buying guides using two proven methods, you can experience better click-through rates and conversions on the products you promote. You can also improve your chances of ranking higher in Google by placing your target keyword in certain locations on the page.

NEXT STEPS

I hope that reading this book has been a great investment of your time. As you discovered, there are many different ways you can increase the click-through rates and conversions on your affiliate pages by making small tweaks to the content and page structure. I encourage you to master the tips and strategies outlined here. By doing so, you can hopefully turn your affiliate site into a more profitable business that can support your financial dreams.

But crafting a good affiliate page that converts well is only half the battle. As you learned in the second section of this book, there are certain affiliate page structures and on-page SEO tactics you can use to help that type of content rank higher in Google. However, that information only scratches the surface when it comes to search engine optimization.

If you'd like to learn more about SEO and how to do it effectively for all types of content on your site, then I encourage you to check out my blog at **seochatter.com/blog**.

On the SEO Chatter blog, I share weekly SEO tips to help you better optimize your content so it ranks higher in the search engines for the keywords you're targeting.

You can also visit the homepage to get the latest SEO news and tips being shared around the web. I pull in the top resources on search engine optimization so you don't have to visit each site separately.

Thanks for spending this time with me and I'll talk to you soon!

Stephen Hockman

ABOUT THE AUTHOR

Stephen Hockman started his first affiliate site in 2008 and earned a whopping $2.18 in the first month. While he couldn't even afford a Starbucks cappuccino with that low of a commission, he still got hooked on the idea of affiliate marketing as a way to make passive income online.

Over the next 10+ years, he consumed every bit of knowledge he could about how to boost his affiliate product sales by thinking outside of the box. He devoured books and online resources on consumer psychology habits, copywriting skills, and website design. He's now an expert in persuasive copywriting, page structure techniques, and conversion rate optimization; the three areas he believes are the most crucial for success in affiliate marketing.

Today, he earns a six-figure income as an affiliate marketer, but that wouldn't have happened without being totally obsessed with research, analysis, and testing of the various strategies and tactics he discovered along the way. At this point in his career, he feels strongly about giving back to the affiliate marketing community by sharing every bit of knowledge he has about making highly profitable affiliate websites.

He's also the creator of SEO Chatter, a site dedicated to sharing daily SEO news and tips to help all types of digital marketers get better at search engine optimization. Hopefully, you'll come to enjoy **seochatter.com** as your favorite place to get your daily fix of SEO strategies you can use to increase your site's rankings and traffic.

DID YOU ENJOY THIS BOOK?

If So, You Could Make a Big Difference!

As you know, reviews are the most powerful way to get people to try a new product. This is especially true for books. Without reviews, it's hard to get people to buy them.

So I'd like to ask you a favor...

Would you please leave some feedback about this book on the Amazon review page?

Honest reviews of this book will not only help bring its attention to other affiliate marketers but it will also help me learn what you did or did not like about the content. I'll be reading the book reviews each week to gain this insight. That way, I can revise the book so that the next edition can be even better and offer more value for everyone who reads it.

Thank you very much!

And good luck on your journey to becoming a better affiliate marketer!

Printed in Great Britain
by Amazon